I0423259

INVESTIGATING THE HAUNTED

INVESTIGATING THE HAUNTED

Ghost Hunting Taken to the Next Level

A Professional Guide to Investigating the Paranormal

*Expand Your Basic Ghost Hunting Knowledge,
Skills & Techniques to Reach "The Next Level"
of Paranormal Understanding!*

Jennifer Lauer & Dave Schumacher

Copyright © 2007 by Jennifer Lauer & Dave Schumacher.

ISBN: Softcover   978-1-4257-8533-8

All rights reserved. No part of this book may be reproduced or transmitted in any form or by any means, electronic or mechanical, including photocopying, recording, or by any information storage and retrieval system, without permission in writing from the copyright owner.

This book was printed in the United States of America.

To order additional copies of this book, contact:
Xlibris Corporation
1-888-795-4274
www.Xlibris.com
Orders@Xlibris.com
41669

Contents

Section I. The Authors

Section II. Introduction

Section III. Who Are You?

Section IV. Theory & Terminology

Section V. Going High Tech

Section VI. Paranormal Investigation, Information and Process

Section VIII. References and Further Reading and Information

DEDICATION

This book is dedicated to all of the members (past & present) of the Southern Wisconsin Paranormal Research Group. Without all of your hard work, support, knowledge, dedication and passion for the field of paranormal research the motivation to write this book would not have been so strong or have such a powerful impact on the lives of everyone involved with this project. Thank you all!!!

Foreword

"Ghost, n. The outward and visible sign of an inward fear."
—Ambrose Bierce, *The Devil's Dictionary*

Ambrose Bierce, clever satirist and self-proclaimed devil's advocate, defined ghosts as mere projections of human emotion. Those who have actually witnessed a hovering apparition in a darkened room would probably disagree with that, but seeing ghosts isn't defining them, either. Whether "haunts" are the surviving spirits of dead people, unknown evil entities or simple figments of overactive imaginations, the one certain thing about them is that they are a mystery to those of us on this side of the veil.

Humans have wondered about the true nature of phantom people for as long as writing has existed, and probably longer. Shakespeare prompted his character, Hamlet, to ponder whether the ghost of King Hamlet was "a spirit of health or a goblin damned." In the Bible, the Book of Luke describes how Jesus' disciples saw his resurrected body and believed they were seeing a ghost. Jesus replied that a ghost does not have flesh and blood.

Neither Shakespeare nor Luke questioned whether ghosts exist. That spirits of the dead live on . . . and may return in some form . . . is a universal belief in human cultures worldwide. Not even modern science has been able to stamp the notion out; TV shows about "ghost hunters" have exploded in recent years and books about hauntings fly off bookstore shelves. Throngs of grieving people have made celebrities of charismatic mediums who claim to be in touch with loved ones who have "passed over." And organized groups dedicated to researching ghost activity have formed all over the world, many documenting their efforts on the Internet. It's possible that the level of public curiosity over ghosts, specters, and assorted spirit beings has never been higher.

Unfortunately, neither has the level of unsubstantiated hype and hysteria. With ghosts everywhere in popular media, "haunted houses" are almost commonplace. The overly suggestible are quick to blame ghosts for every creaking floorboard and rustling curtain. If *every* report is to be believed, our society is in the midst of a runaway, ghostly population explosion. But *can* we believe every report?

Enter Jennifer Lauer and David Schumacher, seasoned investigators of supernatural happenings. After years of dedicated practice, Lauer and Schumacher have learned to utilize electronic instruments along with their own senses in hopes of taking ghost research to a more scientific level. Along with their organization, Southern Wisconsin Paranormal Research Group (S.W.P.R.G.), the pair has developed a stringent protocol for investigations. Their aim is to rule out mundane explanations for footsteps heard in an empty hall, strange whispers emanating from thin air, or misty figures that vanish into shadows, even as they preserve evidence that can't be easily reasoned away.

In this book, Lauer and Schumacher share their know-how with those who wish to go beyond merely sitting in a dark house with a flashlight, waiting for some spooky manifestation to scare them out of their field boots. This is not a manual for the casual thrill-seeker. While their spooky anecdotes do bring chills, Lauer and Schumacher show that scientific research requires training, skill, and most of all, patience. The reward, however, is a data trail of documented evidence, and the chance to contribute more than mere scary stories to the field.

Of course, no matter how much solid data is collected, it's still unlikely that ghosts will ever finally be proven "good spirits or demons damned." That argument will probably rage until the very last human goes to his or her grave. But taking the time and trouble to document and validate these elusive manifestations can make it much harder to discredit the idea that spirits exist. Lauer and Schumacher have laid out precisely how to take that time and trouble. It is up to the reader to follow their lead, set up proper instrumentation and get down to some seriously organized paranormal observation.

—Linda S. Godfrey, author of *The Beast of Bray Road; Tailing Wisconsin's Werewolf* • *Hunting the American Werewolf* • *The Poison Widow; a True Story of Sin, Strychnine and Murder* • *Weird Michigan* • *Strange Wisconsin; More Badger State Weirdness* • co-author *Weird Wisconsin*.

Section I

THE AUTHORS

Chapter 1

ABOUT THE AUTHORS

~ JENNIFER LAUER

I am the Founder and Executive Director of the Southern Wisconsin Paranormal Research Group. This group was organized in 1999 and today is considered one of the most respected and knowledgeable paranormal research organizations in the country. I've been interested in ghosts and the paranormal for as long as I can remember. When I was eight years old my dad took me to see a movie called "Beyond and Back". The movie was about people who had died and came back to talk about their experiences. After that movie, I was hooked. My dad was a huge advocate of the afterlife and we would sit for hours and hours talking about everything from out-of-body experiences, to ghosts, to UFO's, death, E.S.P . . . just a huge variety of different paranormal topics. As I got older, the fascination never left me.

Ever since my dad died in 2004, I feel like there's more of an urgency to know what happens after death. I try to collect evidence to either support the "afterlife" . . . or debunk it. I haven't made any definite conclusions yet, but I don't plan on stopping until I have my proof either way.

~ DAVE SCHUMACHER

I am the Science and Technology Advisor for the Southern Wisconsin Paranormal Research Group. I have also been interested in the paranormal for as long as I can remember. When I was a kid I remember reading The Hardy Boys and The Three Investigators. These books were both fun and informative. The fact that there never really was anything paranormal and it always turned out to be a hoax may have been the roots to my open-minded skepticism. I also have fond memories of investigating the legend of the 'Rat Man' at Adler Park in Libertyville, IL. Many days and nights of walking through the woods in the park kept me both excited and scarred. And then there were the movies, "The Exorcist", "The Haunting", "The Entity", "Poltergeist", and "Ghostbusters". These things drew my interest into the realm of the unknown and they never left me.

My interest (some would say obsession) with the paranormal has only grown stronger as the years went by. However, my interests changed and it was no longer just for fun but it had become more serious. I wanted to know the who, what, where, when, and why of this phenomenon. My approach slowly became more science orientated, which was largely due to my studies in the biological sciences in both undergraduate and graduate school. I wanted to know the truth.

What happens when we die? Is there life after death? Does some part of us and/or our consciousness survive bodily death? These are questions that humans have had throughout the ages. In a way this could be the ultimate quest for knowledge and understanding. The hunger for knowledge and understanding the great mysteries of the unknown is what drives the human race. Therefore, what happens to us when we die is the ultimate unknown. Our mortality becomes more real and apparent as we advance in age. Even if you don't believe in ghosts, you will certainly want to know what happens when you die. So, how can we find out? Well, if you are like me, you want evidence.

I attempt to collect evidence to either support or disprove that there is life after death. No one has any definitive proof either way and that keeps me going. Even though I have been doing this for many years, I don't have all of the answers that I need. However, I plan to keep the quest for the truth alive and well. I guess that is why my favorite quote from the *X-Files* is, "The truth is out there." I believe the truth is out there and I want to know what it is.

Our Qualifications

Ever since childhood, Jennifer and Dave have pursued the paranormal field as a main interest in both of their lives. Individually, they had been investigating and researching paranormal activity for many years until they met in 2002. Ever since, they have combined their talents and experience investigating paranormal activity together and with the other members of the Southern Wisconsin Paranormal Research Group. They have investigated public and private places all over the United States, from huge abandoned prisons and hospitals to private residences. As well as investigating the paranormal, they also hold classes on Ghost Hunting and have been the guest speakers for many paranormal based presentations including historical societies and schools. Jennifer and Dave have both had experience organizing and maintaining paranormal research groups of their own during their professional careers and continue to train and direct other paranormal investigators to bring their intellectual paranormal knowledge to a higher understanding and to what we have been calling, "The Next Level".

Our Inspiration

~ JENNIFER LAUER

The case that really peaked my interest in the paranormal growing up was known as, "The Smurl Haunting". The Smurl home of West Pittston, Pennsylvania, was the scene of a very controversial haunting from 1985 to 1987. The case received a huge amount of media attention and was chronicled in a book and portrayed in a movie both named, "The Haunted". This case was investigated by demonologists, Ed and Lorraine Warren but was later investigated by The Committee for the Scientific Investigation of Claims of the Paranormal (CSICOP). Their investigation revealed this case to be a hoax.

Another case that grabbed my attention while growing up was a local one from Horicon, Wisconsin. In 1987, The Tallmann family—Allen and Debbie; two toddlers, and an infant who lived in a small, three-bedroom ranch house on Larrabee Street reported several strange phenomena which they tracked back to an old bunk bed that was in the children's bedroom. Many reports consisted of furniture flying around the house, blinds going up and down, blood dripping from the ceiling, lights coming on with the power off, writings on the walls, green lights flashing, an apparition of an old lady and flames shooting from their garage.

This case also had a huge amount of media coverage. A quote taken from the Milwaukee Journal Sentinal's interview with the family on Wednesday, January 27 stated that around the beginning of January 1988, the father said the entity made a threat. The quote:

> *"This thing came right out of the floor. It was gassy and foggy . . .*
> *it rose up there and that voice came out of there and it said,*
> *'You're dead.' These green eyes appeared right out of this thing,*
> *and then I saw flames and it was gone."*

In January 1988, I was 19 years old and I remember driving up to Horicon with a friend to try and find the "Haunted House". My friend and I even went to the local library to try and find any possible information on this house . . . but we failed.

This case was never disproved and to this day, remains one of Wisconsin's most famous mysterious paranormal cases.

"The Ghost Hunter's Guidebook" by author Troy Taylor was one of the first books that gave me the inspiration to look at this as more than just a hobby. Besides being an author of over 35 books on the paranormal, Troy Taylor is also the President of the American Ghost Society, a nationally known Paranormal Group. The AGS holds an annual conference every year, which I have attended many times.

~ DAVE SCHUMACHER

In 1984 I remember my parents showing me an incredible picture in the local newspaper. The picture, taken by Fred Shannon of the Columbus, Ohio Dispatch, showed Tina Resch sitting on a chair with a telephone in mid-air flying across her body. The story below the picture described lights going on and off by themselves, clocks stopping and starting, cabinet doors opening and closing, and a variety of objects flying about the home. The famous parapsychologist Dr. William Roll investigated the case. In addition to Dr. Roll, members from the Committee for the Scientific Investigation of Claims of the Paranormal (CSICOP) took a more skeptical approach to the case. James "Amazing" Randi and two scientists from Case Western University were also on hand to get to the bottom of the strange happenings. Dr. Roll claimed the case to be a true example of poltergeist activity (or Recurrent Spontaneous Psychokinesis, RSPK for you science geeks) while CSICOP and Randi said it was a fraud. There is still no consensus whether this was a genuine case of paranormal activity or a hoax. Either way, it was my first serious exposure to poltergeist phenomena and I began my search for other similar stories.

Like Jennifer, "The Smurl Haunting" case fascinated me. I will never forget reading the book "The Haunted" by Robert Curran in my parents' basement (no comments about ghost geeks living in their parent's basement). The story both intrigued and frightened me. Fortunately, my fear quickly gave way for my quest for understanding and knowledge.

A few years later I discovered the movie, "The Entity." This 1983 horror film was based on a real case and is one of the most famous cases in paranormal history. The story was extensively covered in *Omni*

Magazine, Fate, and on the television show Sightings in 1992. I was and still am fascinated by this case. In 1974, Carla Moran began her terrifying experience while living in Culver City, California. She experienced a variety of paranormal phenomena including but not limited to: strange smells, electrical malfunctions, cold spots, and object movement. This may seem bad enough . . . . but it got worse. She also reports being repeatedly raped and beaten by the ghost. It was at this point that she began to seek professional help.

Carla approached Dr. Kerry Gaynor and Dr. Barry Taff. Dr. Gaynor and Dr. Taff were parapsychologists who worked with Dr. Thelma Moss from UCLA. Carla explained her terrifying ordeal. Initially, Dr. Gaynor and Dr. Taff considered the whole story rather unbelievable and seriously thought that Carla needed psychological counseling. However, Carla continued to discuss her horrifying situation with the two parapsychologists and eventually they decided to investigate the case.

When Dr. Taff and Dr. Gaynor arrived at Carla's house, what they saw amazed them. They experienced pops of light, cabinet doors opening and closing by themselves, and a partial apparition form before their very eyes. Using a Geiger counter, they documented background radiation levels dropping to zero when the phenomena occurred and returning to normal when the activity ceased. This is the first case that I know of where radiation levels were measured and why some paranormal investigators continue to monitor radiation levels. The most impressive thing they saw were reverse arcs of light over Carla's head. The lights first started on the walls but then came off of the wall and kept moving in the air. The researchers captured a picture of the phenomena that clearly shows an arc of light over Carla's head and completely off the wall. This photo appeared in *Popular Photography* and it was the first and last paranormal picture to appear in that journal.

Carla Moran moved five times to try to escape her otherworldly tormentor. The phenomena that plagued and tormented her diminished slightly with each move. The majority of the activity ceased after about two years. Because the activity followed her, was centered on her, and pretty much stopped after two years, Dr. Taff and Dr. Gaynor and Dr. Moss thought that this might have been a poltergeist case.

At this point I thought there must be something to all of this and it would be worthwhile to explore further. I craved more information. I wanted to know what a poltergeist really was and what parapsychologists really did. Are ghosts real? Is there any proof of life after death? At this exact point I came across a book that would solidify my interest in this area for the rest of my life.

ESP, Hauntings and Poltergeists: A Parapsychologists Handbook by Loyd Auerbach, published in 1986. This book had it all and a REAL parapsychologist wrote it! It covered the following:

- Apparitions, poltergeists, and hauntings (yes, there is a difference).
- What is a parapsychologist?
- What is psi?
- What is extrasensory perception (ESP)?
- Out-of-body experiences.
- Near death experiences.
- Possible natural explanations for subjective paranormal experiences.
- The impact of paranormal movies on the public's perception of the phenomena.
- Real-life cases.
- How the Amityville Horror was nothing more than wild fiction (what a bummer).
- How to be a paranormal investigator.
- What questions to ask and why.

I think I have read this book at least five times. It gave me my first serious information on the paranormal and how to investigate it. I still refer to it often and I strongly encourage all you would-be ghost hunters and paranormal investigators to read this book.

Personal Experiences—What Keeps Us Going?

According to a recent Gallop Poll 3 out of 4 Americans hold some paranormal belief. Americans are known to believe in extrasensory perception (ESP), ghosts, haunted houses, communicating with the dead, mental telepathy, clairvoyance, astrology, witches, reincarnation, and channeling. This must be pretty accurate, because if it wasn't, we wouldn't be called to do investigations. We have both experienced paranormal phenomena to a certain level that we cannot explain. Some of these experiences were during paranormal investigations and some were not . . . but either way, they have been the experiences that keep us going. Our experiences are what drives us to keep pursuing this field and to make sense out of it all.

~ JENNIFER LAUER

I have had many strange occurrences happen to me that I cannot explain away fully. Looking back, I have found one specific component that has remained the same throughout . . . the majority have all been audible experiences.

Before I ever organized the S.W.P.R.G. I had an experience that still to this day I can't explain. I was 21 years old and had just moved into the house that my grandparents owned while I was growing up. My grandfather, Arthur, died in the front room of a heart attack in 1977 while my 10 year-old brother, John, watched. My bedroom was the same one my grandparents shared for their entire married life. I always loved this room. It was right in the front of the house and had lots of windows and was bright and cheery most of the time. Even at night, the lights from the outside would shine in and make it feel as if it were a warm, cozy, inviting room . . . until one night. I walked into the house around 11:30 pm after my second shift job. Everyone in the house was already asleep. I sat down in the living room and began watching television for a couple of hours before deciding to head off to bed around 1:00 am. That night seemed no different than any other night, until I shut off all the lights, got into bed and started to settle in. Within a few minutes I hear a quick whispery voice talking. I could definitely hear it, but I couldn't understand what it was saying. I not only heard it, but I could feel the warm breath on my ear as it talked. I was suddenly frozen in my bed of fear so I quickly grabbed my pillow and pulled the ends up around my head and covered my ears. Within seconds I heard it again. I felt the breath on my ear just like before, but this time it was as if the pillow wasn't even there. This experience shocked me so much that I never mentioned this to anyone else in the house. Three months later, my mother who lived in the house as well, told me of a strange experience she had the previous night. She proceeded to tell me of the exact same events that had happened to me three months earlier. At that point, I confided in her that it had happened to me as well. To this day, I still cannot explain the exact same experience my mother and I both had in that house. My mother still lives in that house today, but has never experienced it since.

Another experience that stands out clearly in my mind happened during the investigation of the Spaulding House Antique Shop in Janesville, Wisconsin. The Spaulding house property is one of Janesville's oldest reported haunted locations, not to mention the location of the first murder ever recorded in Rock County. Joseph and Lydia Spaulding built the house in 1870. In 1877 Joseph Spaulding actually died in the house, and although

Lydia died several years later in another house in downtown Janesville, all of the telltale signs of this haunting lead to Lydia herself. Most of the past employees of this Antique shop and other businesses that have been on this property swear that Lydia Spaulding IS the ghost that haunts this property.

Our team had been doing a full investigation of the property. It was close to midnight and we had just about exhausted all of our media devices. The owner of the Antique Shop, Tom, and I were standing near the front door about 2 feet away from each other. There was no one else in the room. Our team was in another room several feet away from us finishing up an E.V.P. session when something amazing happened. As I stated earlier, Tom and I were standing about two feet away from each other in a room only occupied by the two of us, when all of a sudden the disembodied voice of a women came up between the two of us and said, "Go Away!" We both heard it . . . plain as day and neither one could explain where this strange voice came from. Was this Lydia? Was she tiring of us and wanted us to leave "her" home? Whatever the reason, this is something that I could not logically or scientifically explain away. Throughout my career as a paranormal investigator, this was the experience that I can't seem to find ANY natural reason for . . . but of course, the experiences don't stop there.

Another audio experience that I was honored to have witnessed occurred at what used to be a place called Manteno State Hospital, in Manteno, Illinois. This hospital has since been torn down . . . yet remains the location of one of the most interesting audio experiences I have ever had. Although MOST of my personal experiences have been just that . . . MY personal experiences, I was fortunate to capture on video/audio tape one of the rarest paranormal occurrences ever.

My team and I were investigating one of the many buildings that made up this huge hospital. We had our Natural Tri-Field meter sitting on a table on the second floor inside the "Dix" building. The audio was turned up on our meter so that we could hear if something entered its field. While we investigated, we had a video camera taping the table with the tri-field meter on it the entire time . . . then it happened! A noticeable dip in the tone of the tri-field meter and then the voice of a nurse paging a doctor from a non-existent PA system. Not ONLY did we capture it on video, but also our investigators actually heard it as it was happening. Now, let me remind you that this place has been abandoned for close to 20 years, there is absolutely NO power running to any of these buildings and the walls are literally falling down around us. No PA system exists in any of the buildings. This wasn't just your average everyday E.V.P.; this had every element possible to use it as factual evidence. It was detected with a natural tri-field meter, it was captured on video and three investigators experienced it all at the same time. What better correlation could you have?

~ DAVE SCHUMACHER

My personal paranormal experiences are few and far between. Two of them involved a specific smell and the other was audio. The interesting thing is that other people who were with me also had the experience.

My first experience happened about eight years ago in November while I was attending a work meeting out on the east coast. We had a few free hours to ourselves and I decided to go for a walk with a co-worker through the historic city that we were staying in. As we proceeded down the street we saw an old church with a cemetery and thought it would be interesting to walk through the old graveyard. About halfway through the cemetery, I smelled fresh lilacs for about two minutes in a small, confined area. The person I was with smelled it as well. We continued to walk and came back to the same spot about five minutes later to see if we could find the source of the lilacs. However, the smell was gone. We could not find any natural source for the smell. No flowers on any graves, no windows open in the church, and it was about 20 degrees out with no leaves on the trees and certainly no flowers blooming anywhere. My next experience, which would be another smell, would not happen for another seven years.

In June 2005, I visited the Ohio State Reformatory. The prison opened in 1896 as a self-sufficient facility for the rehabilitation of male offenders by hard work and education. There were six tiers, twelve ranges with 600 cells. It covered an enormous 250,000 square feet. The six-tier east cellblock is the world's tallest freestanding steel cellblock. The prison hit its highest attendance in 1955 with 5,235 prisoners. However, with changing times and new facilities being built, the inmate population began its eventual decline and most of the prisoners were gone by 1972. In 1983, the building was added to the National Register of Historic Places and completely closed as a functional facility in 1984. The Ohio State Reformatory has been seen in movies such as *The Shawshank Redemption, Tango and Cash, and Air Force One.*

So, why is it haunted? Why would it be any more haunted than any other prison? All prisons have pain and suffering. However, the Ohio State Reformatory seems to have had more than its fair share. Twenty-eight men were hanged between the years of 1885 to 1897 in the Annex at the east end of East Hall. The fate of death row inmates would change from hangings to the electric chair. Three hundred and fifteen people died in the electric chair between 1897 to 1963 at Ohio State Reformatory. As if this was not enough death, more people died at the prison, even those with out an official death sentence met their end in the prison. A fire on April 21, 1930 claimed the lives of 322 people. In 1950, the warden's wife was removing a jewelry box from a closet shelf in the on-site warden's quarters when the pistol fell off of the shelf. The shock of the pistol hitting the floor caused it to fire. The warden's wife was fatally wounded. Within another ten years the warden himself died of a heart attack while working in his office. As one can see, if ever a place would be haunted, this would be the place.

The Ohio State Reformatory offers ghost tours at certain times during the year. The Southern Wisconsin Paranormal Research Group hosted a tour of this phenomenal facility in June 2005. It was about two in the morning when I was walking down a hallway in the warden's quarters with two other people. As we came down the hallway we all suddenly smelled roses. Now, there is NO reason that we should have smelled roses. This place is old, damp and has an overpowering musty/moldy smell. But the smell was there! We followed the smell, which seemed to be moving down the hallway, until it suddenly disappeared. Just as it was gone we turned the corner and came upon ten other investigators. I asked if any of them had smelled roses and they all said, "yes." They had been tracking it for the last thirty minutes or so. We spent the next hour or so investigating that smell. Many times it would come and go and move up and down the hallway and go in and out of various rooms in the warden's quarters. And as before, it would abruptly go away.

Could it have been a sign of the warden's wife? Or was it just because we were all really tired and open to suggestion? Who knows! But it was pretty darn cool. This one is pretty hard for me to explain naturally. I like the fact that we experienced it before we had any idea that the other group of people smelled the same thing. Also, the fact that it moved around the warden's quarters was very interesting!

My most recent experience happened on September 26th, 2005 in Watertown, Wisconsin. The incident involved both Jennifer and I. We had done a full investigation of the home and we were back to go over the findings with the owner. While playing and discussing two E.V.P. that we had captured during the investigation, I distinctly heard five to six loud footsteps on the second floor. Not only could I hear them, but I could feel the vibrations as well! Jennifer looked at me and said, "Did you hear that?"

I said, "Yes" and so did the owner. We bolted upstairs to investigate. There was no one there! We spent some time trying to recreate the situation but were unsuccessful. We went back downstairs and discussed what we had just experienced. The homeowner was very excited and relieved that we had heard that because that was what she was hearing all of the time and now she knew she wasn't crazy!

These are the kinds of experiences that keep us searching for the unknown. They move us, motivate us, and drive us in the direction that keeps us ahead of the pack! Without our experiences, how would we know what to look for?

Guest Author

~ CINDY HEINEN

Cindy is the Electronic Voice Phenomena (E.V.P.) Specialist for the Southern Wisconsin Paranormal Research Group. Cindy first began her study of E.V.P. in 2000. After getting her first successful E.V.P. voice in Gettysburg she was hooked and began her journey into the world of the paranormal. She continued her studies and research independently until 2004 when she was invited to join the S.W.P.R.G. This science based group was a perfect match for her systematic, critical approach to E.V.P. research.

As a member of the S.W.P.R.G. she has helped establish protocol for E.V.P. field recording and analysis. In the S.W.P.R.G.'s Anomalous Research Department she has been active in developing and carrying out E.V.P. based experiments in hopes of better understanding the phenomenon.

Cindy is a long time member of the AAEVP and is a committee member for its Etheric Studies project. She has had the opportunity to present information about E.V.P. in conferences, workshops, periodicals and in research papers.

Section II

INTRODUCTION

Chapter 2

TAKING IT TO "THE NEXT LEVEL"

Congratulations! You have picked up another book on the paranormal!

Walking through the New Age/Metaphysical section of the bookstore, we have seen many books of a paranormal nature. These include such topics as:

- Mystics
- Spells
- Witchcraft
- Tarot Cards
- How to be Psychic
- Cryptozoology
- Big Foot
- The Loch Ness Monster
- UFOs
- Alien Abduction
- Haunted Locations
- Dream Analysis
- The Paranormal
- Haunted Locations
- Ghosts
- How to Hunt Ghosts

While these topics are interesting and fun to read about, a great number of them are purely story-based, anecdotal, or strictly folklore.

This book is related to those topics dealing with ghosts, hauntings and how to hunt ghosts. This book is different. How is it different? Well, let us tell you.

This book was written by two of America's most active, leading paranormal investigators, Jennifer Lauer and Dave Schumacher. They draw upon over 35 years of combined experience of researching, investigating and documenting the paranormal as it relates to ghosts and hauntings. Our investigations uniquely blend science, investigative technique, questioning skills, and psychological and parapsychological information into a successful mixture for a credible, serious paranormal investigation. This book intends to take the reader from a general, "ghost hunter" level to a well informed, analytically thinking, credible paranormal investigator. As the reader, you will gain the knowledge of the author's experiences and use it to go a step beyond to bring the reality of paranormal investigation to a higher level.

In this book, we will tell you what you need to know to be a successful and credible paranormal investigator. We will cover such topics as:

- Proper terminology
- What is a ghost?
- The different types of ghosts and hauntings
- Why should you care about parapsychology and what should you know about the field?
- The truth about orbs
- The equipment—How it works, how to use it, what it tells you and going high tech
- The difference between ghost hunters and paranormal investigators (yes, there is a difference)
- How to conduct an investigation from start to finish
- Provide you with references and other information that will enable you to expand your knowledge of the paranormal

After mastering all of the areas mentioned above, you will be fully prepared to be a successful and credible paranormal investigator. You will be able to have meaningful investigations, collect accurate and important data, help people understand what is going on in their homes and businesses, and help restore much needed credibility to the field of paranormal research.

The Hollywood Hype

Hollywood and the media have really put an emphasis on ghosts and paranormal related topics. Their job is to entertain us, scare us and keep us on the edge of our seats no matter what, but is the true reality of ghost hunting and paranormal investigation being dismissed?

My favorite example of Hollywood's paranormal portrayal gone awry is the movie "White Noise". "White Noise" was written by Niall Johnson in 2005 and stars Michael Keaton as a man who's wife dies and comes back to talk to him through paranormal means. Although this was a fairly entertaining movie, it went terribly awry from the reality of true Electronic Voice phenomena or E.V.P.

The movie started out very well using most of the standards true paranormal investigators look for when working with E.V.P., with tape and digital recordings. Then the movie switched gears slightly and changed its focus to Instrumental Transcommunication or ITC using video equipment. After that, it just lost me completely. The movie was accurate through the first 20 minutes or so into the movie then went completely Hollywood, but of course, that is our personal opinion on how it relates to the real world of paranormal research.

The Sci-Fi show, "Ghost Hunters" tries to walk that realistic tight rope too. Although what they do is pretty close to what the typical ghost hunter does, there is much more that they could be doing that would make them a lot more credible and to set a better example for the paranormal community.

Because they are on television, their viewers (and producers) require visual evidence that is not always possible to provide on command. We don't even know if ghosts can be video taped. They also use a Thermal Imaging Camera, which will track temperatures of objects. On a couple of occasions they have presented evidence on the show of strange, moving thermal images. Using this theory, that would mean that ghosts would have mass and retain some sort of temperature. We can't confirm this, but then again we don't know that it's not true.

"Supernatural", "Most Haunted", "Medium", "Ghost Whisperer" and "Psychic at Large" are just a few of the other TV shows out there which try to represent true paranormal investigators, ghost hunters and psychics. In our opinion, none of these shows represent anything close to what real paranormal investigators do. They are all representative of true Hollywood hype.

People have a tendency to watch things they see on TV and at the movies and accept it as reality. This in turn shapes their beliefs and perceptions. Therefore it is no wonder why people have such a warped view of the paranormal and what paranormal investigators really do. This in turn can damage the credibility of the serious paranormal investigator.

So, it is up to all of us that are serious about the field to correct these misperceptions and beliefs by establishing ourselves as credible paranormal investigators!

Bringing Credibility to the Field of Paranormal Investigation

Why is it important to establish and maintain credibility in the field of paranormal investigation? Well, doesn't it bother you that most people who are interested in this are labeled as ghostbusters (or as we were once called, "phantom finders") at best and "nuts" at worst? Are you afraid to tell your family and friends that you are interested in ghosts and conducting ghost investigations? Are you tired of psychologists and psychiatrists saying that every person who thinks they see a ghost needs therapy and drugs (or is on drugs)? Are you tired of mainstream science saying there is no such thing as ghosts and they will never accept ghost research or parapsychology as a real science? Well, WE CERTAINLY ARE!

Of course, much of the criticism is deserved. There are many people and groups that call themselves ghost hunters or paranormal investigators that are an embarrassment to the field. They pick up one book on where the local haunted locations are, buy a cheap camera, maybe get an electromagnetic field (EMF) meter, pick up a flashlight, and head out to the local cemetery.

Even worse, they are asked to "investigate" a private residence and help the homeowner with their reported haunting and these 'investigators' show up, take a few pictures, wave their EMF meter around and claim there is a ghost. The evidence they claim to prove a ghost is present is a picture with an orb in it and one EMF 'spike' near a fuse box in the basement. Now, they relay this to the homeowner who is now scared out of their mind because these 'experts' have concluded there is a ghost in the house. All we can say is WHOA . . . HOLD ON A SECOND THERE, JOE GHOST HUNTER! YOU'RE KILLIN' ME (no pun intended) AND MY GROUP'S CREDIBILITY!

Doesn't sound very credible, does it? Well, it's not and there are way too many people out there doing this. Now, don't get us wrong, we know that many of these people have very good intentions. The problem is that they are not educated enough in the paranormal field to have taken into consideration all of the possible natural causes for that picture and the EMF reading. Perhaps the orb was just a dust particle or pixilation from a cheap digital camera. The EMF 'spike' could very well be from the fuse box itself. Did they interview the homeowners and other witnesses about the reported activity as to what was happening in the home? Did they know and use their equipment properly? Did they provide any useful information to the homeowner (and we wouldn't consider scaring them out of their mind, good information)? So, how do we prevent this from happening and prove to people that we are serious and credible investigators? Here is what we've done.

The Southern Wisconsin Paranormal Research Group, of which we are both members, is one of the Midwest's most professional and credible paranormal research organizations. This is because of the emphasis the group puts on credibility. When the group was founded back in 1999, it recognized how important and necessary credibility was to the paranormal community and even stated it as the main goal of the organization. The group's byline specifically states: *The goal of our group is to bring credibility to the field of paranormal research and to make a concerted effort to display the best evidence and information that is possible.*

. . . And we have accomplished this by doing the following:

1. Believer vs. Science vs. Cynic
We have kept an open mind or what we like to call healthy skepticism. We don't believe everything nor do we discount all data that suggests paranormal activity. There is certainly no consensus on what a ghost is, but there is plenty of speculation. We feel that people certainly do have subjective paranormal experiences but what those experiences are and how they perceived them are certainly open to debate. We are definitely willing to entertain the possibility that there is life after death. Heck, who doesn't? However, we do try to rule out every possible natural explanation first, and this is done without being ridiculous. If you discount everything using natural explanations, even when that natural explanation is more improbable than a paranormal one, then you become one of those dreaded

skeptics. The more appropriate term for those people would be a cynic. So, considering all possibilities and not ruling out anything will go a long way in establishing your credibility both to those people who believe and those who do not.

2. Scientific Methods

If you say you are science based, then use science. Science is NOT just using fancy electronic equipment and walking around taking thousands of photos. The hardcore skeptics have a field day with this. Being scientific involves much more and can be rather boring and dull at times. When trying to gain new knowledge of something, the scientific method or scientific process is basic to the investigation. You use observations and reasoning to develop possible explanations for the observed phenomena. This is called a hypothesis. Once the hypothesis is formed, you test predictions that come from the hypothesis by doing a variety of experiments. The experiments should be repeatable. Now, once the hypothesis has been confirmed repeatedly by experimentation and research, then it becomes a theory and new predictions are based upon it.

All aspects of the scientific method are subject to review by other researchers. Here is a general guideline to follow:

1. Define the question
2. Get information
3. Develop a hypothesis
4. Research/experiment/observe
5. Analyze the data
6. Interpret the data and draw some conclusions (which may lead to a new hypothesis)
7. Tell people about your results and let them analyze the data and try to replicate your results

Research and observation can involve looking into the history of a location or reviewing published literature for information (both natural and paranormal) and cases like those you are working on. Members of the Southern Wisconsin Paranormal Research Group are constantly reviewing new books, journal articles, and products. We also develop hypotheses and test them in the field. Hopefully, one day, this will lead to the development of a paranormal theory that can be validated over and over again both by ghost researchers and mainstream science. Knowing your stuff and applying the appropriate scientific terminology and really using the scientific method will go a long way in making you appear legitimate.

3. Investigation Skills

You must have good investigation skills. This entails knowing how to interview people, knowing the right questions to ask, how to relate to people, how to know when someone might be stretching the truth, how to listen, and paying attention to details. Another big attribute is patience. We have spent hundreds if not thousands of hours sitting and waiting for something to happen. Then you have to add in all of the time it takes to review the hours and hours of video footage, electronic voice phenomena (E.V.P.) recordings, environmental readings, and other data that you collected during the actual investigation. This may seem like a lot, but it isn't really any different than what a police investigator or crime scene investigator does when working on a case.

4. Equipment Use

You have to know how to use the equipment, it's limitations, how it works, what it measures, what the readings mean, and what types of natural things can give readings. Equipment should be used in conjunction with good investigative skills and witness testimony. The reason for this is there is no piece of equipment that is a certified ghost detector. Therefore, you can't use equipment and it's readings as proof of a ghost. We do have data to which certain equipment readings have correlated with locations where people have experienced ghostly phenomena. This includes such things as transient 'spikes' in the electromagnetic field when an apparition is present, steady higher than normal background readings in the electromagnetic field in residual hauntings, drops and/or increases in the background radiation levels, and higher than normal positive ion counts. This is meaningful data, but only if you first rule out any natural things that can effect the equipment. The bottom line is that others will take you more seriously if you know how to use your equipment, know what it means, know what natural things can affect it, know it's limitations, and know how to interpret the data.

5. Education

Be well versed in the literature. This includes ghost hunting, investigative skills, psychic/metaphysical, religious, psychology, perceptual psychology, anomalistic psychology, and parapsychology.

Now you might be asking, why do I need to read about psychology and parapsychology? It may seem academic and boring but you will need to be aware of the theories, concepts, and terminology. It will also help you determine when someone is not having a paranormal experience and they are misinterpreting or misperceiving something. For example, it is a known fact in psychology that people who are under a lot of stress have a much lower tolerance for ambiguous situations and therefore tend to misinterpret things. On the other hand, if you are familiar with the parapsychological literature, you may think about a possible case of Recurrent Spontaneous Psychokinesis (RSPK) or what is typically called a poltergeist. Parapsychologists have determined that poltergeist activity is due to a living human agent that is under a lot of stress and they are releasing this stress subconsciously via RSPK. So, your knowledge of psychology and parapsychology would help you determine what might really be going on in the example above. I have found a variety of good materials in academic journals and books, magazines, and on the Internet. One of the best quotes from the movie *Lilo and Stich* is, "Knowledge is power and I like power." Knowledge is power! It gives you the power to interpret and understand what might be going on and thereby make you very credible in what you do.

6. Client Care

Realize that if people call you to investigate their home or business they are probably looking for help. Of course it is good to collect all of your data and tell them what you found, but remember, nine times out of ten they are looking for help. They are looking for someone to explain what is going on, determine that they are not crazy, and/or make the situation go away. Here is a recent case we worked on as an example. A homeowner contacted the S.W.P.R.G. because they had a variety of things going on in the house such as objects moving, someone being pulled out of bed by an unseen force, animals behaving strangely (including the unexplained death of one of the pets), footsteps being heard on the second floor when no one was there, and many other odd occurrences. The homeowner was very distraught as one might imagine. We went to the home three times: once for the pre-investigation, once for the full investigation, and the last time to discuss our findings. While reviewing a few E.V.P. with the homeowner, we all heard five heavy distinct footsteps on the second floor. Not only did we hear them, we felt the vibration from them. At this point we all rushed upstairs to try to find a natural explanation for what we had just experienced. After some time investigating and experimenting, we could come up with no natural explanation for what had just happened. When we sat back down at the table the homeowner looked at us and said, "I am so glad that you heard that. That is what I hear all the time and now I know I am not crazy." We provided her with some information and are still in contact with her today to help her understand and deal with her experiences. Yes, it was great to collect some data, get some E.V.P. and experience the footsteps. However, the thing that made us look great to the homeowner was that we experienced what she had been experiencing and provided her with information about the phenomena and that alleviated some of her fear.

7. Choosing Cases

The final thing you need to know (and do) in order to be credible is to know when to either not take a case or tell the client that you can't help them and it might be better to talk with a qualified professional such as a doctor or counselor.

There are two main reasons that you may have to do this. The first one is that there is certainly the possibility that people are not experiencing anything paranormal and that they may have a mental disorder or another medical condition. Unless you are a licensed doctor or counselor, do not try to help this person. Besides, that sort of activity is illegal. This is both for their best interests and yours. It is also for your safety. People with mental problems can pose serious physical, mental and legal risks to you. The second situation in which you might suggest that they seek help is when there is paranormal activity in the home. People who see an apparition or experience a residual haunting are scared! The unknown can deeply affect people and when you can't understand something you become afraid and the fear can lead to stress. Another paranormal situation would be that of RSPK. Parapsychologists believe that RSPK is due to stress and that stress is being released subconsciously via RSPK. Both of these examples show that people may need the help of a qualified individual in order to deal with their stress and fear. The hard part is finding a professional in the medical field that won't immediately label them as "nuts" and start them on all kinds of medication. It is helpful to try to find someone who, at least, has a working knowledge of parapsychology and psychic phenomena. We have been able to get some good people to refer these folks to from the Parapsychology Foundation and the American Society for Psychical Research. If you don't try to pretend that you are something that you are not and therefore don't get in over your head, you have truly helped someone and maintained your much-deserved credibility.

Well, there you go. You know what you are in for when you read this book. So, pick yourself a comfortable spot, grab a drink, keep an open mind, and let us take you to the next level of paranormal investigation!

Section III

WHO ARE YOU?

Chapter 3

GHOST HUNTER, PARANORMAL INVESTIGATOR, OR PARAPSYCHOLOGIST— WHO ARE YOU?

Cue *The Who* . . . .
"Who are you? Who? Who?

This song nicely summarizes the content of this chapter. Ghost hunter, paranormal investigator, or parapsychologist—who are you?

These labels have been used and interchanged for many years by those investigating ghosts and hauntings. A quick search on the Internet proves this point. Are these terms interchangeable? Not really. The inquiry into ghostly phenomena has been going on long enough that differences in how people do things, what they think, what they believe, how they use technology, how they interpret data, and their overall level of interest has led to apparent differences in people's level of interest and what they call themselves.

Individuals who study ghosts and hauntings can be placed somewhere on a sliding scale with ghost hunters being at one extreme and parapsychologists at the exact opposite. Paranormal investigators are positioned somewhere in the middle. It should be understood that there is variation even within each classification. For example, ghost hunters can be on the hobbyist level where they mainly go out just for fun to take pictures, spend time with friends, and try to have a paranormal experience. The serious ghost hunters will spend more time at it, use a variety of equipment, and research and document activity the best that they can.

A review of what each of the following involves will help you determine who you are and who you ultimately want to be in your pursuit of the paranormal.

The Parapsychologist

Parapsychologists study experiences which are not within the area of known human capabilities. These experiences include ESP, PK, and survival. They attempt to explain the phenomena within the context of mainstream science using the scientific method. If they can't, then they propose new hypotheses that are an extension of known science. The majority of this research takes place in the laboratory under extremely controlled conditions. The results of their research are published in peer reviewed scientific journals.

Parapsychologists have advanced graduate degrees in parapsychology, but more frequently in psychology or other disciplines with an emphasis (i.e.: thesis project) on a parapsychological topic. For example, Michael Persinger is a neuroscientist but explores parapsychological topics.

Though parapsychology has its root in investigating ghosts and hauntings, most parapsychologists don't do much these days with ghosts and hauntings. There are very few that do field-based investigations and when they do, it is usually part of a planned research project. So, they are not what most people would consider a ghost hunter.

Now with this information, the reader may be asking what parapsychologists do in regard to ghosts and hauntings?

Parapsychologists are interested in people who experience ghosts and hauntings and would like to determine what characteristics and beliefs they have that enable them to have paranormal experiences. They explore the possibilities of ESP and PK and how they relate to and could possibly explain subjective paranormal experiences. They have also taken RSPK agents into their lab in order to better understand their abilities in controlled conditions and to see if the RSPK agent can consciously control their PK.

In addition to studying people, they study different environmental factors such as EMFs, GMFs, contextual cues, Local Sidereal Time, etc . . . that could play a role in ghostly activity. They consider not only the possibility that a ghost may interact with and change the environment but the possibilities that: 1) changes in the environment cause people to have an experience and/or 2) that people can affect the environment (ie: PK and RSPK). This could go a long way in explaining ghostly experiences.

In respect to the survival question, parapsychologists are interested in determining what consciousness is and if it survives and continues after bodily death. Once this has been determined, only then can we begin to 'hunt' ghosts. Therefore, it is obvious that they don't approach the field with the biased belief that ghosts definitely do exist.

So, as one can see, parapsychologists are not ghost hunters and ghost hunters are not parapsychologists. Parapsychologists are mainly science-based academic researchers.

The Ghost Hunter

This is the term that most people are familiar with. The vast majority of books, television shows, movies, and news media refer to people who investigate and research ghostly activity as ghost hunters.

What is a ghost hunter? What do they do? What do they believe? How do they go about 'hunting' ghosts? These are some of the questions to be pondered in this section.

The ghost hunter can cover a range of involvement in itself, from the hobbyist to the more serious hunter. It seems as if the majority are somewhere in the middle. They go to public and private locations to experience the paranormal, take a picture, use some basic equipment, and record E.V.P. Some do more complete investigations that involve multiple visits to a location, asking good questions, and trying to find natural explanations for the phenomena. Regardless of the level of involvement, ghost hunters are out to hunt ghosts.

The question that comes to mind is how do you *hunt* for *ghosts* if we are not even sure that they exist?

According to the Merriam-Webster Online Dictionary, hunt is defined as:

To pursue for food or sport;
To pursue with intent to capture;
To search out;
To drive or chase especially by harrying;
To traverse in search of prey.

This definition of 'hunt' does a pretty good job of helping understand what a ghost hunter is and does (except for pursuing for food—we haven't heard of anyone go after a ghost in order to eat it, but it probably wouldn't have many calories if one was somehow ingested).

If one is going to hunt something (ie: a ghost), then one has to assume that it exists. The majority of ghost hunters believe that ghosts exist and strive to collect evidence during their investigations to prove to themselves and others that ghosts do exist.

Setting out with the assumption that ghosts do exist poses the following problems:

1. The existence of ghosts is not fact; it is a belief at this point in time.
2. Since we don't even know what consciousness is, how can we know if it continues on after bodily death?
3. There is no equipment or technology designed to detect ghosts.
4. We don't know how a ghost would interact with our physical world.
5. Going in with the belief that ghosts exist could lead to a biased interpretation of the data collected. This bias can be anything from saying every orb is a ghost (and never dust) to discarding negative (but yet important) data if it does not prove that ghosts exist.

Therefore, this sets one up to make what statisticians call a Type I Error—accepting something that isn't so. On the other hand, one shouldn't dismiss everything as natural explainable phenomena or they could be making a Type II Error—missing something important (ie: missing true paranormal phenomena).

So, how do we strike a balance between these two things? How does one critically investigate the paranormal and collect the best information and evidence possible?

Enter the paranormal investigator . . .

The Paranormal Investigator

The term "paranormal investigator" can include anyone who investigates anything paranormal—ghosts, aliens, UFOs, etc. But let's assume for the sake of this book that the paranormal investigator is investigating ghosts and hauntings. However, the information could apply to a paranormal investigator that is researching the other prior mentioned phenomena.

Paranormal investigators are something between a ghost hunter and parapsychologist, taking the ghost hunter to the next level. A few of their characteristics are:

1. Very serious and treat it like a job
2. Attempt to rule out all possible natural explanations
3. Make no assumptions and don't assume that ghosts exist
4. Utilize the latest equipment/technology
5. Use investigative techniques
6. Have an excellent working knowledge of the relevant literature—paranormal, parapsychological, psychological, etc
7. Science and investigation based
8. Critical thinkers
9. Inquisitive
10. Open-minded

Now, this doesn't mean the ghost hunter won't have these traits too. It's just that the paranormal investigator advances them to the next level and applies them to their investigations.

Besides these characteristics that many people have, what do paranormal investigators do? Here are a few things that make them unique in their paranormal work.

They use investigative techniques when doing their work. Witnesses are separated when interviewed, they ask open-ended, probing questions; stories between witnesses are matched up and corroborated, all facts are checked—not only with the ghostly activity but time of day, conditions at the time, who was there, etc. All of these things are critical when gathering and analyzing reports of paranormal activity.

They utilize parapsychological and psychological information in their field research/investigations. One example of this would be giving clients the AT-20 question set. This would help determine how they tolerate ambiguous situations. If one finds out that they don't tolerate ambiguous situations well, then perhaps the investigator could examine the possibility that the client misperceived and/or misinterpreted some natural phenomena. Another example would be an investigator being well informed on current paranormal hypotheses. Not only does this help figure out what might be going on, but also it provides the opportunity to test a hypothesis and contribute to the advancement of the field.

They use a science based critical approach when doing investigations. This includes collecting data (perhaps data logging), analyzing data, looking for correlations in the data, looking for correlations between your data and that collected by other groups, accepting and putting forth your data—even if it doesn't support the existence of ghosts (no file drawer effect), and asking if your data supports a normal or paranormal explanation. Another very important thing is to be open to the evaluation and criticism of your data by others. This is how things progress in all other fields!

They develop and test hypotheses. This includes not only testing hypotheses developed by other groups and researchers but also developing and testing your own hypotheses. Also, there are many ideas and beliefs within the paranormal field that have very little if any data to support them. A few of these that the S.W.P.R.G. Research Team has examined are: Does increased geomagnetic activity increase the quantity of E.V.P.? Does the natural EM meter really ignore all man-made fields and thereby only detect ghostly activity? Do haunted locations have magnetically distinct features that places that are not considered haunted do not have? Looking at these things will give us a better idea of what a haunting is and how to approach an investigation.

Another aspect of this is attempting to recreate a reported paranormal event during an on-site investigation. Doing this can help determine if the phenomena was perhaps just something natural that was misinterpreted.

They provide meaningful, understandable, and accurate information to the public and media. There is a lot of bad information out there about the paranormal. This leads people to a misunderstanding about the field and what we do. It is also a major contributing factor to people's fear of the paranormal. Therefore, it is the job of the paranormal investigator to provide correct information in order to set the record straight!

They provide the client with the information they need in order to deal with the phenomena. Remember, people are calling you because they want to know what is going on and how to deal with it. Collecting data is good, but helping the people who contacted you is the most important thing. Staying in contact with the client and helping them deal with the situation until they no longer need you or the phenomena stop is an excellent way to show you are a credible and caring paranormal investigator. Not only will this help the client but also it will provide you with more data and an opportunity to see the case progress. This, in return, may help you with future cases.

Well, there you are! Do you now know who you are? Do you know what level you want to beat? Remember, whatever level you are at there is always room to learn more and advance!!!

Section IV

THEORY & TERMINOLOGY

Chapter 4

WHY SHOULD I CARE ABOUT PARAPSYCHOLOGY?

What is parapsychology? Why should I, the paranormal investigator, care about it? What do parapsychologists study? What type of information from parapsychology can be used to help with a paranormal investigation?

The serious paranormal investigator should be able to answer each of the above questions and if not, then the time to learn the answers is now.

Knowledge of parapsychology is essential for the paranormal investigator. The major reasons it plays such an important role are:

- Parapsychology used to be known in the early days as psychic research, which started out investigating mediums, psychics, and spiritualists. There was also considerable time spent collecting, investigating and analyzing cases of ghosts and hauntings (or what most parapsychologists would term spontaneous cases).
- The majority of research in parapsychology is now done in the formal psychology lab setting. Unfortunately, ghosts have yet to make themselves available for a controlled laboratory study. Therefore, most of the investigations into ghost and haunting cases fall into the arms of amateur paranormal investigators and ghost hunters.
- The information gained during research by parapsychologists can be used when investigating ghosts and hauntings. This also works the opposite way in that good quality information collected during field investigations can be a starting point for parapsychologists to set up and do certain laboratory experiments.

- Amateur paranormal investigators and ghost hunters are NOT parapsychologists. Parapsychologists have advanced college degrees and usually hold faculty positions at universities and/or at other formal research laboratories. Also, the majority of parapsychologists would not be considered ghost hunters or paranormal investigators. Some do investigate spontaneous cases but usually do it as a somewhat controlled field experiment in an attempt to collect data that can be used to support a hypothesis they are testing.
- Finally, if you do believe in the possibility of ghosts then the field of parapsychology can provide some possible mechanisms by which these entities are able to manifest, communicate with, and influence things in our physical world.

The History of Parapsychology

The historical roots of parapsychology can be found with the mediums that were predominant during the 1850s with the Spiritualist movement in Europe. These mediums claimed to be able to contact the dead, channel loved dead relatives, levitate objects and themselves, produce ectoplasm, and make apparitions manifest. These spectacular claims drew the attention of well-known and respected scholars and researchers who wanted to investigate these claims.

E. Dawson Rogers, a spiritualist, wanted to build credibility and respect for the mediums and others of the spiritualist movement. This seemed like an excellent opportunity for the spiritualists and the scientific community to work together. Thus, the Society for Psychical Research (SPR) was formed in 1882 in London. Soon afterward the American Society for Psychical Research (ASPR) was formed in 1885. The two societies began their investigations of paranormal phenomena.

The majority of early psychical investigation and research involved testing the abilities of mediums and others with self proclaimed psychic abilities. Many frauds were discovered through rigorous, science—based investigations. A skeptical attitude spread through the scientific members of the SPR and ASPR, which led to conflict with the Spiritualists. With the scientists becoming more and more skeptical and the spiritualists holding on to their beliefs, a deep rift separated the two sides and the Spiritualists abandoned the SPR and ASPR. However, despite this split, investigations into life after death continued and expanded extensively.

The SPR and ASPR continued with its original work of investigating those who claimed to have psychic abilities. Both organizations, especially the SPR, expanded their research into other areas. They began to collect, investigate, examine, and analyze spontaneous cases of apparitions, ghosts, poltergeists, crisis apparitions, out-of-body experiences, and apparitions of the living. The result of this work was the publishing of a two volume set in 1886 titled, *Phantasms of the Living,* by Edmund Gurney, Frederic Meyers, and Frank Podmore. Though this was a significant contribution to the field, there was still a lack of research-based science with proper statistical analysis to explore and explain paranormal phenomena.

Modern science based experimental parapsychology came into being with the development of certain statistical tools and the work by Joseph Banks Rhine. This was the time when the term parapsychology became widely known and used instead of psychic research.

J.B. Rhine joined the Duke University psychology department in 1929 and redefined the field of parapsychology with a variety of firsts in the field. He was the first to employ rigorous scientific experimentation to the study of psi phenomena, which lead to greater respect of the field in science and academia. He also founded the parapsychology laboratory at Duke University. This parapsychology lab at Duke University is still open today as an independent entity and is known as the Rhine Research Center.

During his time at Duke, J.B. Rhine did many experiments dealing with extrasensory perception (ESP). His early and most well known experiments were those involving guessing cards. Initially he used a normal deck of playing cards. However, it was difficult to analyze the results from normal playing cards since the analysis could look at the proper suit, color, and numerical value. Therefore, Dr. Rhine wanted a simpler set of cards to use.

Dr. Rhine collaborated with Dr. Karl Zener, a psychologist at Duke. Dr. Zener suggested using some simple symbols. Thus was the creation of the well known ESP cards (or what were originally called Zenner cards). There are fives cards with each having only one of the following symbols: square, circle, plus sign, star, and wavy lines. The cards were used for experiments on clairvoyance, telepathy, and general ESP. Dr. Rhine also developed a statistical test that would tell if a subject's performance differed significantly from chance.

So, through the use of five cards with symbols and some statistical tests, Dr. Rhine revolutionized the field of parapsychological research.

Parapsychology was and still is an active field of research. For example, Project Star Gate in the 1970s and 1980s was funded by the Central Intelligence Agency and the Defense Intelligence Agency to explore remote viewing as a way to gather intelligence from a safe and comfortable couch in a laboratory in the US. Also, in the 1990s, the Defense Department funded more remote viewing experiments. These days, scientific lab research is now mainly found in psychology, neuroscience, medical, and anomalous psychology laboratories.

So, where do you go if you want to learn about or study parapsychology?

There are few if any schools that offer degrees in parapsychology. There are a few that offer an emphasis in parapsychology while pursuing a traditional psychology degree. The major institutions are:

University of Edinburgh, Edinburgh, Scotland (UK)
The Koestler Parapsychology Unit

University of Hartfordshire, Hatfield, England
The Parrot-Warrick Research Unit

University of Amsterdam, The Netherlands

Princeton University
Princeton Engineering Anomalies Research School of Engineering/ Applied Science (PEAR)

There are other organizations that offer courses and/or a certificate in parapsychology:
The Rhine Research Center

Certificate Course in Parapsychological Studies
Loyd Auerbach, instructor
HCH Institute, Layfayette, CA

These institutions and courses will provide you with the knowledge that you would need to seriously study the various areas of parapsychology. The next section will cover what parapsychology is and the specific areas included within the field.

What is Parapsychology and What Does it Involve?

Parapsychology is the study of "apparent anomalies of behavior and experience that exist apart from currently known explanatory mechanisms that account for organism-environment and organism-organism information and influence flow."
—*Parapsychological Association, 1989, pp.394-395*

Parapsychologists attempt to explain the phenomena within mainstream science. If the phenomena can't be explained within the context of mainstream science, then new hypotheses and theories are proposed that are an extension of known science. A variety of these hypotheses about ghosts and hauntings are presented in chapter 5. Some of those ideas may seem well outside of mainstream science but new data, experiments, and information will continue to support or not support those hypotheses. For example, new information gained in the study of quantum physics gives new possibilities for explaining paranormal phenomena with the context of science.

The variety of different areas and experiences within the field are collectively termed 'psi' and are represented by the symbol ψ. Psi is synonymous with psychic and psychical. The three aspects of psi are:

- Extrasensory Perception (ESP) or what some term Extended Sensory Perception. This area of psi is considered informational or receptive psi.
- Psychokinesis (PK). This is psi as an interaction. It is when the mind has a direct affect on an animate or inanimate object. Telekinesis is the older term used to describe this phenomena of moving distant objects with one's mind but most parapsychologists just refer to it as PK. To make it simple, let's just say it is mind over matter.
- Survival. This is the life after death area that all ghost hunters and paranormal investigators have come to know and love. However, it includes much more than just ghosts and haunting as you will see in the following paragraphs.

Now, let's take a more in depth look at what is involved in each of these three aspects.

ESP

Extrasensory perception entails various 'powers' that enable one to receive information without the use of the five senses. No one is really sure how this information is transmitted or received but parapsychologists have classified the following types of ESP.

Telepathy

It is common for people to jokingly say that, "I know what you are thinking." This is known as mind-to-mind communication and is the ability to be aware of the information, thoughts, feelings, and emotions of another person. People who have this ability are commonly referred to as mind readers. Experiments in this area have been going on for some time. Another interesting set of experiments are those that involve dream telepathy.

Clairvoyance, Remote viewing, or Remote Sensing

This is the ability to receive information about objects or events at the present time. Though visual perception of the information is most common, it can also include feelings, auditory, and olfactory (smelling) sensations. Researchers today tend to label this phenomenon as anomalous cognition.

Psychometry

Psychometry is the ability to 'read' the history of an object or a location. The idea is that the object or location being 'read' has recorded an imprint of some past event and some people are able to pickup that information when they hold the object or are in the location.

Retrocognition

This is the ability to gain information about events in the past without using the five known senses or inference. This is an alternative to psychometry that is slightly different in that retrocognition does not involve reading the recorded history of the object or location. It seems as if the location or object may simply serve to focus one's attention on the task at hand, which is to gain information about past events.

Precognition

This is the opposite of retrocognition. It is the ability to receive information about things in the future. This may be somewhat harder to accept and explain since we are dealing with future events. No one knows if the future is predetermined. Even if it is, then how does that information travel backwards in time? Another problem involved in research in this area is how do we know for sure that information is being received precognitively? It could also be possible that we decide on an outcome and psychokinesis is used to influence the outcomes of certain events to give us what we want.

Psychokinesis (PK)

Psychokinesis is an interesting phenomena that can be divided into two categories depending on the size of effect. Micro-PK involves effects that occur on a very small scale down to possibly the microscopic and/or atomic level. Obviously these effects are not visually detectable so one needs to observe the results with the aid of computers, statistical analysis, or other advanced equipment. Examples of micro-PK would include test subjects attempting to affect the output of random number generators so the results are no longer random. These types of experiments are the most common in the parapsychology lab since they are easy to conduct, control, and interpret.

Macro-PK includes effects that occur on a large scale and can be seen. One of the most well known examples of this is the spoon bending made famous by Uri Geller. Other phenomena considered to be at the macro-PK level include: psychic healing and psychic surgery (however, there seems to be micro-PK that can occur as well); materialization and dematerialization of objects; teleportation, which is the movement of objects across a certain distance without the object moving through the space between where it was and where it ended up; the imprinting of images on film or video (also known as psychic photography); and the imprinting of sounds and voices on tapes or other recording devices. And finally, there is poltergeist activity, more formally known as Recurrent Spontaneous Psychokinesis. This could be considered to be the macro of all macro-PK level activity.

Survival

Ghosts and hauntings are extensively covered in other sections of this book. However, there are other areas that parapsychologists study in order to determine if there is life after death. So, let's briefly look at some of these other subjects in the realm of survival related phenomenon.

Mediums and Channeling

The first area that deserves mention includes mediums. Now, one could argue that this should be included under the ESP section since that would explain more about how they receive their information. Still, mediums claim to be able to communicate with the spirits of people who have died so they make a good way to study the survival phenomena.

Mediums can be differentiated into three different types. The first include the physical mediums, which are able to receive verbal messages from the dead and produce physical disturbances during their sessions. The physical disturbances can be levitation, object movement, and knocking or rapping. The second category of mediums are the mental mediums. These mediums speak with the dead mainly by going into a trance and becoming 'possessed by the dead person's spirit and a control entity. The third and final class of mediums are the psychic mediums. These are similar to but slightly different than the mental mediums in that they do not go into a trance and remain fully conscious during their communications with the spirits. Well known psychic mediums include John Edwards, James Van Praagh, and Sylvia Browne.

Another more vague and encompassing term that includes mediums is channeling. Mediums are said to channel the spirit of the deceased. However, channeling also entails contacting and communicating with non-human entities such as aliens and other dimensional beings.

Another survival related phenomenon that involves mediums is automatic writing. This is when the medium's hand writes a message without the conscious control of the medium. It is thought that the medium's hand and/or mind are being guided by the spirit of the deceased.

Out-of-Body Experiences (OBE)

OBEs are very similar to clairvoyance and remote viewing except that the person having the experience feels as if they leave their body. This enables them to view their physical body as well as the rest of the world around them. In the metaphysical world this has been called astral projection and the reports are very similar except those describing astral projection report being tethered to their body by a silvery cord.

Reincarnation

Reincarnation involves the soul or disembodied consciousness of someone who has died being reborn in another person or even an animal. Reincarnation is a strongly held belief in Eastern religions such as Hinduism and Buddhism. The strongest evidence for this is when very young children remember a past life of which they should know nothing, and have not been exposed to the information. This phenomenon is studied by collecting information from the people who claim to have been reincarnated and then trying to verify the facts of the case.

Near-Death Experience (NDE)

People who are clinically dead for a short period of time experience this phenomena. They report a similar sequence of events in the majority of the cases reported. This includes the following: hearing a buzzing noise; having a sense of peacefulness; leaving one's body; traveling through a tunnel towards a bright light; meeting dead relatives, friends, and/or religious figures; seeing one's life pass quickly before their eyes; and a feeling that this is a truly wonderful experience which they don't want to end. The interesting thing is the main aspects of the experience seem to be similar across different cultures. There are slight differences that mainly concern the type of religious figures present in the experience.

It is possible to attribute the NDE to brain states triggered by cardiac arrest and anesthesia. Also, the patients may not have been truly dead since there was still electrical activity in the brain. Other arguments against the paranormal nature of a NDE are that NDE type experiences have been triggered in living people by the following: severe psychosis; drug usage such as LSD and DMT; electrical stimulation of the temporal lobes and thus the hippocampus; and decreased cerebral perfusion which results in cerebral hypoxia. This is a common condition for jet pilots that experience incredible forces when going extremely fast and vertical.

However, it can be argued that if the experience is truly due to neurochemistry of the brain, then why are the experiences all not exactly the same? Why are the experiences very specific to the individual? These are questions that can only be answered with future research.

Induced After Death Communication (IDAC)

A new therapy discovered by Dr. Allan Botkin, which is used by psychologists as a therapy to reduce trauma, stress and grief, could be a new area for survival-related research. It involves using eye movement desensitization and reprocessing (EMDR). Dr. Botkin revised the EMDR and called it 'core-focused EMDR.' Dr. Botkin discovered that during the core-focused EMDR that patients could be induced to have an IDAC by following a specific sequence of events. The IDAC allows people to deal with their grief by enabling them to communicate and reconnect with their dead loved ones. Dr. Botkin has pointed out that IDACs have much in common with NDEs and spontaneous after death communications (ADCs). Even though the paranormal nature of IDACs is uncertain, it does provide yet another avenue for exploring the possibility of life after death.

Obviously, there is much useful parapsychological information that the paranormal investigator should be aware of in order to be credible when considering all possibilities.

Chapter 5

GHOSTS, HAUNTINGS AND
PARANORMAL HYPOTHESES

There are many theories as to types of ghosts and hauntings and what a ghost is. These range from simple beliefs to scientifically researched hypotheses. A few examples are:

- Dead people
- Residual energy
- Aliens/portals
- Recurrent Spontaneous Psychokinesis (RSPK)
- Fraud
- Black or white magic
- Mental or health problems
- Gods, devils, demons, angels, spirit guides
- Animal spirits
- Ancient gods
- Hallucinations
- Visual illusions
- Misperceptions and misinterpretation

So, what do we really mean when we say a location or object is haunted? What type of phenomena do we consider indicative of a ghost? Haunting? Poltergeist? Are there different types of ghosts and hauntings? While some people freely interchange the terms ghost, apparition, haunting, and poltergeist, most parapsychologists and serious paranormal investigators differentiate these terms and phenomena. This chapter will attempt to explain these differences.

Ghostly type paranormal activity can be classified under three main categories:

1. Residual haunting/haunting/place memory
2. Apparitions (including apparitional haunting)
3. Poltergeists (Recurrent Spontaneous Psychokinesis)

Haunting Questions

Has anyone ever recovered any physical evidence left by a ghost? No. Has it been proven that a ghost has a solid physical presence? No. How can ghosts affect the physical environment that we live in if the only thing that survives bodily death is the spirit or some energetic form of consciousness? If a ghost has no solid physical mass then how can a picture of one be taken? How can a spirit with no mouth, tongue, or vocal chords produce sounds on a recording device? These are a few of the many fascinating questions that need to be answered. However, there are some possible explanations when one looks at a variety of possible explanations.

Residual Haunting

The first category is the residual haunting. The more recent term is place memory. The identifying characteristics are:

- The phenomenon is independent of the people in the location. There is no interaction at all between the ghost and the living.
- It can go on for decades if not centuries.
- It almost never includes object movement.
- People can experience visual, auditory, olfactory (smell), and/or kinesthetic (feeling or a sense) phenomena.
- Apparitions witnessed in a residual haunting are different than the true "dead guy" apparitions (see the next section). The apparitions in a residual haunting are more appropriately referred to as pseudo-apparitions or apparition-like phenomena.
- One person, a few people, or all people in a group may experience the phenomena.

A family member shared a story of a haunting of this type. They said that each night around 7:00pm the entire family would hear the back screen door open and the sound of footsteps would shortly follow. The ghostly footsteps could be heard going from the back door to the stairs and then they would proceed up the stairs and eventually fade away. This would happen over and over again each and every night! There was never any interaction between whatever came in the back door and went up the stairs and the family members. This is pretty much a classic example of a residual haunting.

The current hypothesis accepted by most paranormal investigators is that the environment (being a location or object) can record highly emotional (both good and bad) events. The activity is imprinted on the environment much like an image or sound is recorded on a video or audiotape. Those events with higher emotional content seem to be recorded and perceived better. Then, under the right environmental conditions (magnetic fields, electrical charge, weather, or who knows what) and with the right person, the recorded event is re-played and perceived. You can simply think of it as a looped video playing over and over again.

Investigators with the S.W.P.R.G. as well as others have noted electromagnetic fields (EMFs) and geomagnetic fields (GMFs) that are higher than background levels. The fields are somewhat consistent though they may have frequency and amplitude modulations (more on this later). Some skeptics contend that these phenomena are due to the EMFs and/or GMFs causing one to hallucinate. However, this does not explain how different independent witnesses see, hear, smell, or feel things that have the same accurate historical context.

Considering Other Psi-based Explanations

Psychometry is a possible explanation for residual hauntings. It is thought that certain objects and locations may record highly emotional events, though the process by which this would occur in unknown. Then, when someone enters the location or touches the object, the recorded event is replayed and perceived by the percipient. The total experience would entail the proper 'sensitive' person to be in the right place at the right time with the proper environmental conditions in place (whatever those may be).

Retrocognition is another potential explanation that is similar to psychometry but somewhat different. The percipient is getting the information directly from the past and not from the imprint 'recorded' in the location or object. Instead, the object or location would be used as a point of focus for the percipient.

PK from the living percipients may be responsible for object movement and other physical events observed during a residual haunting. This is rare but it has been known to occur. Since residual hauntings are thought to be just a recording and do not involve the surviving consciousness of a dead person, PK from the living percipients would be one of the only ways that various objects could be moved. Think about it this way, while watching a recorded video you can hear and see everything recorded on the video. But, if the guy on the video told you to turn the lights down so you could enjoy his movie better, it would be up to you to carry out that task.

Apparitions

The second category includes apparitions of the intelligent type. These are the ghosts, spirits, souls, dead guys or whatever you want to call the part of the human consciousness that survives bodily death.

The identifying characteristics of apparitions are:

- They display some sort of intelligence and interact with the percipient.
- Object movement is rare but possible via apparition mediated psychokinesis.
- They are usually visual but can also be a voice, smell, sound or sensation.
- The duration can vary.
- The apparition looks like a person. Sometimes they are solid and sometimes see-through. It is common to not realize you are witnessing an apparition until it disappears. People have sometimes reported the figure to have fuzzy edges.
- Age and physical appearance can vary depending on how the apparition wants to project itself to the percipient.
- One person, a few people, or all people in a group may perceive the apparition depending on the intent of the apparition and/or the sensitivity of the percipients.

G.N.M. Tyrell describes four types of apparitions [1]:

1. Apparitions of the dead (those dead for more than 24 hours). These are also known as 'post-mortem' apparitions.

2. Crisis apparitions. These are the result of a dangerous or crisis situation.
3. Apparitions of the just dead (12 to 24 hours) or dying. They appear to people who have some sort of emotional attachment to them.
4. Apparitions of the living. Some refer to these as doppelgangers or bilocations. The spontaneous cases are when it just happens with no effort by either the sender or percipient. Then there are the experimental cases. This not only includes the formal lab setting but also those when someone tries to project himself or herself. Out-of-body experiences (OBE) are also of the experimental type but, only when the OBE sender is perceived by the percipient.

Though this classification scheme is rather old, it still holds up well today and all cases of apparitions can be classified in one of the above categories.

The S.W.P.R.G. investigated the historic Spaulding House in Janesville, Wisconsin in April 2003. Joseph and Lydia Spaulding built the house in 1870. Joseph died in the house on August 12th, 1877. Many different people have reported ghostly activity at this location. The following is just a partial list of what has been experienced while the house was being used as an antique shop:

* Lights would go on by themselves.
* The heat would be mysteriously turned up in the ladies room.
* Papers and files would fly off a desk.
* Glasses and dishes were heard rattling.
* Footsteps were heard going up and down the stairs.
* Running water has been heard in the ladies bathroom on multiple occasions. However, no water was present in the sink when someone checked.
* People have smelled freshly baked bread.
* People have smelled cigar smoke on multiple occasions.
* The front door alarm was activated on numerous occasions. The owners asked the ghost to stop doing that at one point and the alarm did not sound again for about two and a half hours.
* A customer in the store felt a cold hand on her shoulder.
* A customer felt pressure on her hand and felt as if something was guiding her by holding her hand.
* Multiple customers have heard whispering in their ears.

- One person heard what sounded like a child's voice say, "Mommy."
- Two people on the second floor heard a voice say, "Get out!" And . . . . they left.
- One customer saw a mist.
- A customer witnessed the apparition of a woman wearing clothing that looked to be from the 1800's.
- Another customer saw the profile of a woman in Victorian clothing.

Something interesting happened to one of the investigators and the owner towards the end of the investigation. They both distinctly heard a voice say, "Go away." No one else in the group heard the voice and the tape recorders running at the time did not pick it up.

It is very possible that this was an intelligent apparitional haunting. Why? Well, the entity seems as if it was trying to get people's attention and responded when asked to stop doing something. It is also interesting that two different people at different times heard a voice say about the same thing, "go away" and "get out." In addition, at least two different people saw what appeared to be a woman in Victorian clothing. The key here is that it seems that the apparition was interacting with people by trying to get their attention and/or telling them to go away!

How do people perceive apparitions? Why do only some people see an apparition while others in a group do not? Why are there not any good or consistent photos of apparitions? Why don't apparitions leave any physical evidence? Is there a hypothesis or model that can explain all of this?

Frank Podmore originally proposed that apparitions are the result of telepathically induced hallucinations. G.N.M. Tyrell expanded on this idea and his model, the 'idea-pattern' model has held up fairly well over the years.

The 'idea' is a piece of information originating from the 'agent' and is sent telepathically to the percipient. This information is received in the subliminal/subconscious levels of the percipient's mind where it is processed to create an apparitional 'drama'. Tyrell described a 'mid-level' of consciousness that was responsible for elaborating on the basic telepathic message. This would eventually lead to the construction of an appropriate visual image to convey the message. Tyrell likened this to the producer and carpenter of the theatrical type.

Telepathy could explain why sometimes an apparition is seen only by one person in a group and other times by everyone in a group. It seems as if it is just up to the ghost to determine who and what the people will see.

Additional support for this idea comes from cases of crisis apparitions. It is thought that the person in the crisis situation reaches out telepathically to someone they are emotionally attached to. Of course one could argue that clairvoyance, OBEs, or remote viewing could be another possible explanation for crisis apparitions. So many possibilities and so few pages . . . .

Now remember that there is no proof that ghosts have any type of physical mass that could be used to interact with and affect objects in our environment. Yet, there are numerous reports of object movement, feelings of being touched, voices recorded on recording devices, and anomalous pictures associated with apparitions. How can this be?

The answer may be with PK. PK by the ghost and/or living people involved in the situation may account for the physical activity associated with apparitions. Another similar possibility is that the fear of the apparition could induce stress within the living and they could be initiating RSPK activity.

So, there might not be a dead guy involved at all. It is very possible that the living are simply creating the apparition and its associated activity by telepathy and PK. PK could also be used by the living to 'project' an apparition into the physical environment.

More support for this psychokinetic ability is seen in the next section on poltergeist phenomena, also known as *Recurrent Spontaneous Psychokinesis* (RSPK).

Poltergeists (RSPK)

The third main category is poltergeist phenomena. The appropriate terminology these days is Recurrent Spontaneous Psychokinesis (RSPK) and was originated by William G. Roll. This phenomena is different from the first two described in that the activity is centered around and produced by a living person called the agent.

The identifying characteristics of RSPK are:

- Limited duration of a couple of weeks to two years
- Noises such as rappings and footsteps
- Object movement
- Objects disappear and reappear in unusual places
- The appearance and dropping of small rocks on the roof

- Electrical items will malfunction and/or go on and off by themselves
- Phone malfunctions
- Unexplained computer problems
- Small fires break out
- OCCASIONALLY visual apparitions are seen (which would be the pseudo-apparition or apparition like type), voices are heard, and strange smells are detected.

The agent that the activity is centered around is under some sort of stress and the RSPK is the result of the subconscious mind releasing the stress. The agent is often an adolescent girl but can be male and even an adult. They are unaware that they are causing the phenomena. The phenomena will cease rather quickly once the agents realize that they are responsible and deal with the stress.

The phenomenon itself is centered on objects or areas that are symbolic of the cause of stress. This focusing can occur in three possible ways:

1. "area"-focused
2. "object"-focused
3. "individual object"-focused

A recent case the S.W.P.R.G. investigated provides an excellent example of the symbolic focusing of activity.

A family and their daughter who was in her early twenties contacted us. The young woman had a small child and was currently working in the food service industry at a local hospital. She had previously been involved in an abusive relationship with a former boyfriend and was now thinking of making some changes in her life.

The daughter was tired of the food service job and certainly did not want to cook anymore, especially when she got home. She was spending time on the computer looking for colleges when the activity seemed to progress to the worst she had experienced. She claimed that the kitchen floor began to vibrate and shake like there was an earthquake, the kitchen cabinet doors opened and closed by themselves, and she had previously heard footsteps in the kitchen and hallway outside the kitchen. In addition (as if this was not enough) she heard the sound of a baby crying. Needless to say, she was upset and described herself as having an anxiety attack. This is when she and her family decided to contact the S.W.P.R.G.

During our investigation we discovered she had a bad experience the last time she attempted to start college classes. She wanted to pursue a career in the medical field but needed to work around her schedule and that of her small child. She definitely did NOT want to neglect her child. The college counselor told her that she would need to commit more time than she could and that perhaps she would be better off doing something such as food service or other menial labor. She was very upset with the counselor and it would be a few years later before she would even contemplate going back to school.

Based on this information, it became clear what was going on. The RSPK was due to the following:

- The baby crying was symbolic of the daughter not wanting to neglect her child.
- The activity in the kitchen was symbolic of her unhappiness in the food service business and not wanting to cook when she was home.
- The trigger was using the computer to look for colleges. Based on her past experience with school, this stress triggered the RSPK and was directed at and symbolic of the stress and concerns she had.

The young woman did not want to accept this possible explanation and wanted to believe a ghost was causing her problems. She was dissatisfied with our explanation and cut-off communication with the S.W.P.R.G. Therefore, we do not know if she ever accepted what we said and if the activity ceased.

Upon reviewing the environmental data (EMF, GMF, radiation, and temperature), there was nothing of interest found. This is in agreement with what others have found. RSPK phenomena seem to yield little if any changes or trends in regards to EMF, GMF, radiation, and temperature collected at the location of the activity.

There is data that shows RSPK activity is associated with changes in the geomagnetic field. It seems as if sustained increases are not needed but rather just changes in the geomagnetic field are sufficient [2-4]. So, it is beneficial to keep track of the geomagnetic data by using the aa-index or Kp-index.

There is also data that shows that some RSPK agents have symptoms of subclinical epilepsy with associated epileptic seizures (based on EEG). An

EEG of some subjects indicates possible complex partial seizures (CPS), especially if certain spikes on the EEG were slightly more pronounced [2, 5-6]. The similarities between CPS and RSPK are somewhat interesting:

- Both are involuntary
- Both are recurrent
- Both involve some sort of energy release
- Both peak in the early teens
- Both involve emotional expressions
- Both can be triggered by changes in the geomagnetic field
- Both involve sensory perceptions (hallucinations with CPS)
- Some of the visual hallucinations associated with CPS are similar to those reported in RSPK cases

The most common type of seizure experienced by those with temporal lobe epilepsy is a CPS. Researchers have also noted correlations between reported paranormal experiences and temporal lobe signs, which have been studied using specialized question sets and EEG [7-8]. Therefore, based on this information and the similarities between RSPK and CPS, it would be advisable to determine if the RSPK agent has a history/diagnosis of temporal lobe epilepsy or has ever experienced a seizure.

More Haunting Hypotheses

Haunting hypotheses can be assigned to one of three major groups:

1. Hypotheses that include natural or non-paranormal explanations.
2. Hypotheses that are psi or paranormal based.
3. A combination of 1 and 2.

Natural Hypotheses

These explain paranormal phenomena in purely normal terms using known scientific principles. They draw upon established theories from psychology, physics, neurobiology, etc. The following is a list of these natural hypotheses:

- Trickery/fraud. Yes, unfortunately this does happen. The motivation may be anything from not wanting to accept responsibility for breaking something to attempting to get media attention to drive business. But whatever the reason is you must be able to determine if someone is trying to pull one over on you.

- Incomplete/false memory. People don't always remember things the way they actually happened. Remember the old telephone circle game you would play as a kid? Once the story gets back to you, is it ever the same? Most likely it is not. It may help to recreate the situation when the phenomena occurred. Also, get multiple witness testimony if you can.
- Mental illness. There are a variety of mental illnesses that can cause people to experience all kinds of abnormal (and what we may call paranormal) phenomena. Since most of us are not psychologists or psychiatrists we need to know when we can't help these people and refer them to the appropriate person. However, remember that even some of the craziest stories may have some merit. If you suspect any sort of mental illness I would suggest you proceed with caution if not decline to take the case all together.
- Natural explanations that people may just not know about. This might include things such as: air in the water pipes that causes banging sounds; drafts and pressure changes that cause doors and windows to open and close; cars, trucks, and trains that go by outside; and a house that is settling.
- Some of the more obscure natural explanations would be: subterranean water sources that cause sounds and vibrations; low level seismic activity; infrasound waves which have been found to cause the eyeball to vibrate when the sound wave is at a frequency of 18 to 19Hz; electrical discharges that can sound like footsteps and knocking; magneto restriction that can lead to object movement; electroforms which can cause ghost lights and other luminous shapes; Peltier effect that can lead to cold spots and hot spots; Page effect which can give bangs and explosive sounds; and magneto phosphenes leading to dancing lights.
- Prolonged fear and stress can cause people to hallucinate. Ask people what their fears of the paranormal are and if they have been under any more stress than normal.
- Human perception/misperception and interpretation/ misinterpretation. Human perception and interpretation is very complex and involves many factors. We use one or more of our five senses to perceive something and then our brains interpret that information. Our interpretation is based on previous

knowledge, experiences, and beliefs. Therefore, different people can interpret things that are perceived differently. In addition, there is something known as tolerance of ambiguity and ambiguous stimuli. Intolerance of ambiguity is generally defined as the tendency to perceive ambiguous stimuli as threatening or fear inducing [21]. Studies have shown that people with a fear of the paranormal have a low tolerance of ambiguity [18]. Therefore, it might be worthwhile determine what the tolerance of ambiguity is for the people experiencing the phenomena and this can be done with a simple questionnaire [19].

- Attentional bias is another interesting phenomena in psychology. Events go unnoticed because they are not important. Then for some reason or another we become interested (perhaps from a suggestion or expectation) and there is a gradual increase in the frequency of 'paranormal' events. Basically, every little noise is noticed and labeled paranormal while in reality it is just another everyday sound, which would usually go unnoticed. This is more formally called the attentional and "perceptual contagion effect" and has been shown in an experiment by Houran and Lange [20]. The power of suggestion and expectation also adds to the above-described psychological phenomena. So, if someone tells you a place is haunted and you WILL hear and see things when you go there, then you will have the expectation and the belief and more than likely you will perceive something and label it paranormal. However, it is very possible that you are experiencing something very normal but are labeling it as paranormal because of your expectations, beliefs, attentional bias, and intolerance of ambiguity.

There are at least three problems with these natural explanations. First, one hypothesis explains one thing (like a strange sound) while another is good at explaining something else (seeing things). So, most of the time, you would need to draw upon a couple of different hypotheses to explain a single haunting case. Second, they don't take into account the history of the location. Third, one would think people would have different experiences when interpreting natural phenomena since we all have different backgrounds, beliefs, and experiences to frame our interpretation. So, the question is then, why do different people who have no prior knowledge of a location with different backgrounds and different beliefs ALL have the same experiences? This is why one needs to look for other explanations . . . those of a more paranormal nature.

Other Possible Paranormal Hypotheses

The top five current hypotheses in the parapsychology world are:

1. The Neurological Hypothesis, which says that exposure to certain environmental factors or energies or certain frequencies can affect the brain. This in turn causes the one to hallucinate [10-13]. So, if ghosts and hauntings are made up of certain electromagnetic fields, then perhaps our brain picks up on these frequencies and interprets them by hallucinating an experience.

2. The Perceptual Hypothesis, which says exposure to certain environmental energies affects brain functioning. This will allow one to perceive events or objects, such as ghosts, that we can't normally perceive. This is also known as Budden's Electro-Staging Hypothesis [9]. Budden proposed that electromagnetic fields have a hallucinogenic effect. These 'fields' enable us to see something that is always there but hidden because the 'fields' are not present. In addition, Budden felt that certain types of electromagnetic fields could sensitize individuals to further such fields and render them 'psychic.' This could explain why people who have one experience tend to have more and more experiences. This would certainly be an interesting alternative to the experience induces belief and belief induces experience phenomena in traditional psychology.

3. The Telepathic Hypothesis, which says that telepathy affects brain functioning [14]. This is the idea discussed above from Podmore and Tyrell.

4. The Psychokinetic Hypothesis, which says intense subjective experiences can intrude on the physical world [5, 17]. Basically, if one sees an apparition in their mind (a hallucination with or without an environmental trigger) then this may lead to physical changes in the environment. This would include things moving, temperature changes, changes in EMFs, etc.

5. The Ghost Hypothesis, which says that apparitions are genuine independent entities that can be directly perceived or independently detected as anomalous energetic effects [15-16]. This would be the part of the human consciousness that survives bodily death and

retains its intelligence. People refer to these as ghosts, spirits, souls, apparitions, or phantoms.

Natural and Paranormal

Finally, there is the combination of paranormal and natural, which probably happens in a majority of the cases. Parapsychologists have gotten a small, but significant number of results in the laboratory setting. Support for this idea comes from pseudo-poltergeist activity and the unhaunted house diary study [20]. Perhaps there is an actual paranormal experience that has a paranormal explanation. However, this can scare people and put them on a state of high alert. Then, every little sound or event that is somewhat obscure will be interpreted as due to the ghost. It becomes very difficult to determine what is paranormal and what is normal.

As one can see, there are different types of ghosts and hauntings and an abundance of hypotheses that attempt to explain them. The only thing that we know for certain is that no one has all the answers. Only through further research and investigations will we obtain the knowledge to determine which, if any, of the above information is correct.

Psi and Paranormal Investigation Data

So, how can one take pictures, record video, or record audio of ghostly activity if there is nothing that we know of that is physically present when a ghost is around? Once again we can look to PK.

Parapsychologists have conducted many experiments with individuals attempting to imprint images on unexposed film. While some fraud and deception was discovered, there were a few individuals that could produce unexplainable anomalous images on the unexposed film. Therefore, since it seems possible that the living are able to create anomalous photos, it could also be possible for them to use PK to create E.V.P. and video anomalies.

The question then becomes, are the recorded anomalies due to the PK of the ghost or the PK of the living people involved? Could it be due to both? These are questions that deserve to be addressed through proper research and analysis.

It is interesting that it seems as if people who have been conducting E.V.P. sessions for a longer period of time get more consistent results. Also, E.V.P. can be easily recorded in locations that have no history of a haunting or ghostly activity. So, is it possible that the person conducting the E.V.P. session is actually imprinting sounds and words on the recording device by PK? Anything is possible when it come to this field. It also makes one pause and question the usefulness of using E.V.P. as proof of a ghost.

Another thing to think about is how many photographs, video, or audio anomalies have been captured when no one is around? A review of this type of data and some experimentation by the many groups out there could help determine if the PK induced anomalies are coming from the dead guys or the live guys.

It is obvious that there are many possibilities when considering the many different mechanisms that may explain various ghost and haunting phenomena.

The Truth About Orbs

Orbs here, there and everywhere!

Eventually you will stumble across the topic of orbs no matter where you go for paranormal information. Orbs were and still are a hot topic of debate among paranormal investigators. There are a variety of hypotheses on what they are, where they come from and why they are captured on cameras. Let's not spend time on speculation, but instead why don't we explore what we do know about orbs.

There are three main views on orbs [23]:

1. The rationalist view—All orbs have a natural explanation.
2. Minority belief—Some orbs have a natural explanation while others have a paranormal explanation.
3. Rejection-of-rationalism—All orbs are paranormal.

Those who hold the rationalist view believe that all orbs have a natural explanation and there is no link to the paranormal. Natural causes of orbs include:

1. Stray reflections (often from a high powered flash close to the lens) from shiny objects in the environment are re-reflected off of the lens surface. This can even occur without a flash! All it takes is just a light source and/or shiny object that reflect light into the camera lens.

2. There is diffraction from the flash reflecting off of dust, dirt, pollen or other particles near but no on the lens [22].
3. The phenomenon known as 'blooming.' This is the bleed-over from one pixel to another [24]. This is mainly attributed to the older and lower mega pixel digital cameras.

Recently, the above three have been termed the orb zone [23, 26, 27].

Support for the orb zone theory comes from two studies done by researchers in the UK. The results were [23, 27]:

1. There was *no* difference in the number of orb photos between haunted and non-haunted locations.
2. Increasing the depth of field increased the number of orbs.
3. There were more orbs while using a flash in low light conditions compared to not using a flash under the same conditions.
4. Increasing the distance of the flash from the camera lens resulted in fewer orbs.
5. The 35mm film camera had fewer orb pictures then digital camera pictures.
6. There were fewer orbs when using a higher mega pixel setting versus a low mega pixel setting.

One can see that the data strongly supports the view that all orbs are *not* paranormal and most can be attributed to natural causes. However, there are a number of questions that remain about the possible paranormal nature of orbs.

What about orbs captured without a flash or when no reflections or reflective surfaces are present?

What about orbs that are partially hidden behind a solid object, especially those outside the orb zone?

What about orbs that people claim to see with their eyes?

How about the possibility of orb pictures created through psychokinesis? A living person or a ghost could do this. There is prior work on PK imprinted images (psychic photography) where some individuals have been able to imprint images on unexposed film. So, this is definitely a possibility that needs to be explored.

Therefore, it is possible that some orbs are paranormal (minority belief) since the above questions still need to be answered.

An investigation done by the S.W.P.R.G. of the Bar Next Door in Madison, Wisconsin provides an example of a moving orbic anomaly that may be paranormal in nature.

The Bar Next Door has a long history of paranormal phenomena. Employees and patrons have reported hearing footsteps on the stairs, the feeling of being followed, rattling glasses, lights turning on and off by themselves, seeing shadows of people, doors slamming closed, chairs being moved and seeing the apparitions of a man and woman. At one point during the investigation there were various EMF spikes and dips recorded on the second floor at the same time that an anomaly was captured on video in the basement. The speed of the anomaly was calculated based on the distance traveled and the number of video frames it was seen recorded in. It was moving at a speed of 68 mph and it was in the same location where employees had previously reported seeing an apparition and feeling extremely uneasy!

We are still unable to provide a natural explanation for this orbic anomaly that correlated with changes in the EMF and was in the same location with various reports of paranormal activity.

While the majority of orbs have natural explanations there are still some instances where no natural explanation can be found. Therefore, the best thing to do is take every precaution you can to prevent false positives. This includes:

- Moving the flash away from the lens.
- Control the environment by reducing or eliminating dust, moisture, reflective surfaces, etc . . .
- Apply an antireflective lens coating.
- Use baffles that will trap stray reflections within the lens.
- Take pictures of the same area with two different cameras in different positions and/or use at least one 35mm film camera.

Eliminating false orbs will make you and your group more credible and assist in determining if any orbs are paranormal in nature.

Section V

GOING HIGH TECH

Chapter 6

THE EQUIPMENT—GOING HIGH TECH

Every ghost hunter and paranormal investigator has a plethora of meters and other gadgets they use on investigations. This includes such things as: EMF meters, thermometers, cameras, video cameras, motion detectors, gaussmeters, digital recorders, and much more.

Why do people use this equipment? What does it detect? What is the best way to use it? What do the readings mean? Do they detect ghosts? Is using this fancy equipment considered science? Where should the equipment be placed? What are the pieces of equipment that have shown somewhat consistent results during haunting and poltergeist investigations? Why is data logging important?

These are some of the many questions that will be addressed in this chapter. However, this chapter will not review each and every piece of equipment that one could possibly use. Nor will it explain exactly how to go about using it. It is assumed that the reader has a basic knowledge of the various different pieces of equipment used during investigations, what they measure, and their proper use.

Now, with that being said . . . Let's talk tech!

In the Beginning . . . There was Harry Price

In the 1930s a man named Harry Price came onto the ghost hunting scene. He is considered by many to be the father of ghost hunting. He is also credited as to having the first ghost hunting equipment set, which included:

- Measuring tape
- Thread
- Camera
- Chalk
- Powder
- Tape
- Notebook
- Mercury

Though simple, this equipment enabled him to gain much information on ghosts and hauntings.

His intelligence and excellent investigation skills helped him accomplish many things in the field of ghost hunting without a vast array of high tech equipment. Think about this for a few minutes, how much more information has our advanced equipment of today given us? Do we really know more about ghosts now then Harry Price did? Much of the equipment used today is simply a more advanced form of Price's equipment.

What does that tell you? It says that the most important piece of equipment is . . . YOU!

The Investigator—The Most Important Piece of Equipment

Yes, you, the paranormal investigator is the most important piece of equipment in an investigation. All the technological equipment in the world won't help a person who is a poor investigator and who doesn't know how to use the equipment they have or is unable to analyze and interpret the data.

Remember, *people* have paranormal experiences. Without people, there are no experiences. Equipment can be used to detect, quantify, and qualify environmental anomalies at the time of a subjective paranormal experience, but they *can't* tell you what that experience was to the people having it.

So, if you . . .

- Use your brain
- Use your investigation skills
- Use deductive reasoning to look for natural explanations for the phenomena experienced
- Analyze and interpret the data you collect properly

• Pay attention to your personal experiences and those around you

You will be the most important piece of equipment on an investigation.

Ghost Detectors?

None of the equipment used by ghost hunters and paranormal investigators was designed to detect ghosts. They were designed for other uses. Also, we don't know what a ghost is or how it could interact with our physical world. Therefore, we have two strikes against the equipment right out of the box.

Now you are probably asking, why did I just waste a few hundred dollars on a bunch of worthless equipment? Don't worry . . . your money was well spent and there is a reason to use the technology that is available to us.

Using a variety of different equipment to detect changes in the environment is advisable since we don't know what a ghost is or how it interacts with our world. People have reported a variety of changes in the environment when they've had paranormal experiences. These perceived changes in the environment include: temperature drops, a feeling of heaviness in the atmosphere, feeling that the environment is charged with energy, feelings of a high amount of static electricity, electrical problems, and objects moving. These are things that can be objectively measured with cameras, video cameras, EMF meters, thermometers, etc. So, it is safe to say that we can attempt to validate these changes in the environment by objective measurements with the equipment we have available to us.

The changes that are measured may or may not be anomalous in nature. But, in order to determine if they are, we need to collect the data and see if there are correlations between changes in the environmental conditions at haunted locations when someone is having a paranormal experience. Once we determine if there are any correlations with paranormal phenomena, then we can begin to determine what the cause of that change in the environment is. Another way to put it is: the ghost interacting with and changing the environment or are natural (but strange) changes in the environment causing people to have a paranormal experience?

Correlation vs. Causation

Many people believe that ghosts interact with and change the environment when they are present. They believe that ghosts are made of or manipulate EMFs in order to manifest. Others believe that ghosts draw upon heat (warm air) in order to manifest and this drawing of heat causes cold spots. Basically, they have already decided that the ghost is causing the environmental changes. But, is the ghost really causing the changes? Have we established that there is a definite correlation between paranormal experiences and environmental changes? What else could cause these changes in the environment?

The Merriam-Webster Online Dictionary defines correlation and causation:

> *Correlation—a relation existing between phenomena or things or between mathematical or statistical variables which tend to vary, be associated, or occur together in a way not expected on the basis of chance alone . . .*

> *Causation—the act or process of causing; the act or agency that produces an effect.*

Based on those definitions and the things discussed previously, we are still in the mode of collecting data and determining what environmental changes *correlate* with paranormal activity. Making the jump to saying that a ghost caused the readings on the equipment is premature because:

- There have been inconsistent results. One example is EMF readings. Some reported haunted locations have variable EMF readings while another does not. Or one group reports temperature drops while other investigators have never objectively recorded a temperature drop. What leads to these inconsistencies? Read on.
- Use of different equipment and different methods. Let's look at the EMF meter again. There are so many different EMF meters (single axis, multi axis, natural EM meter, different frequency ranges, etc) that it is hard to make any overall conclusions. In addition, people use different methods of collecting data-collecting data with the main power on vs. having the power off, data logging over time in one area vs. walking around and writing down readings, etc . . . There are so many variables here that it is hard to draw any definitive conclusions.
- Improper use of equipment. Examples include walking around with the Natural EM meter, pointing the IR thermometer unknowingly at a cold window, taking pictures in front of reflective surfaces,

not establishing baseline readings, using a different meter when repeating measurements in a location throughout an investigation, and on and on and on.

- Improper interpretation of the data. This includes but is not limited to lack of determining all of the natural causes for the readings.

Therefore, we are at best still in the stage of collecting data to determine if there are correlations between certain environmental changes and paranormal phenomena. This will continue to be the case until there is some sort of standardization of the paranormal investigation method, the type and quality of equipment used, and its' proper use.

Science and the Scientific Method

Many groups and investigators claim they do research and use science and the scientific method when conducting their investigations. The problem with saying that is, simply walking around with equipment, taking readings, and saying a ghost is present is NOT scientific. To say one is doing science would entail taking it to the next level:

- Science would be determining what is and what is not detectable by the devices used.
- Looking for an explanation of what is being detected is doing science.
- Developing and testing hypotheses is doing science.
- Using the scientific method is doing science.

The definition of the scientific method from *Wikepedia.com* is:

> *"Scientific method is a body of techniques for investigating phenomena and acquiring new knowledge, as well as for correcting and integrating previous knowledge. It is based on observable, empirical, measurable evidence, and subject to the laws of reasoning. All the evidence is collectively called scientific evidence."*

There are four main steps in the scientific method:

1. Observe and describe the phenomena of interest.
2. Form a hypothesis to explain the phenomena.

3. Use the hypothesis to predict the existence of other phenomena and to predict the results of new observations.
4. Do properly designed and performed experiments to test the predictions. Independent researchers can repeat the results of these experiments.

If the experiments prove the hypothesis, then it may become a theory. If the experiments do not prove the hypothesis then the hypothesis must be rejected or modified.

The key to the scientific method is the predictive power of the hypothesis or theory based on experimental tests.

Now, many people claim that science doesn't have all the answers and studying the paranormal is outside mainstream science and it will never be accepted so there is no point to trying to use science to explore and explain the paranormal. It is true that science doe not have all the answers and that studying the paranormal is *currently* outside of mainstream science. However, the methods of science can be easily applied to paranormal research. Even though the phenomena is not currently accepted by most of the scientific community, using the scientific method when doing paranormal research and investigations will allow one to correctly collect data, form and test hypotheses, and therefore be more credible within the field. So, there is a place for science in the paranormal and subsequently a place for the paranormal in science!

Equipment Placement

Where does one setup their equipment? Where do you take EMF readings? Seems like those are stupid questions, right? Perhaps not.

It is obvious that the camera system should cover any and all areas where things have been reported. In addition, various equipment readings should be taken in the locations where the phenomena was said to be. This is especially important if object movement was reported.

Another location to take readings in is where the person was when they experienced the phenomena. This is important because it is possible that ghostly phenomena are hallucinated experiences that may or may not be caused by something paranormal. Regardless if it is paranormal or not, there may be some environmental changes in the location where the people were when they experienced the phenomena. These environmental anomalies may have affected the person's brain and/or body in a way that led to the experience. It is possible that ghosts affect the environment in a way that sends a signal to the percipients brain that enables them to have the paranormal experience. Recall the earlier discussion about Tyrell's telepathically induced hallucination. Exploring environmental readings in locations where people were during their experience will help shed further light on this hypothesis and others in regards to how and why people experience ghosts.

It is also good to take readings in these locations in order to rule out any natural causes of the phenomena. There have been numerous cases where people have reported seeing a ghost at a certain time of night when lying in bed. After ruling out a waking or sleeping dream, what else could it have been? Well, many of these experiences turn out to be nothing more than EMF triggered hallucinations with the EMFs coming from clocks and radios close to the person's head when they are lying down. Of course, if no readings are obtained then you can begin to look for other causes.

In summary, it is important to take environmental readings both in locations where people claim the phenomena was AND in locations where they were when they experienced the phenomena in order to get a more complete and accurate picture of what happens in the environment during paranormal experiences.

Why the S.W.P.R.G. Uses the Equipment it Does

The S.W.P.R.G. decides to use certain pieces of equipment for the following reasons:

1. It seems logical to explore changes in the environment based on what people have reported during paranormal experiences.
2. The review of scientific literature leads to field-testing, experiments, and use of certain pieces of equipment.
3. Prior investigations by the S.W.P.R.G. and other investigators have shown possible correlations between the data collected by certain pieces of equipment and reported haunted locations.
4. The data collected with certain pieces of equipment seems to be somewhat consistent between haunted locations.
5. Correlations have been seen between equipment readings and when people report a subjective paranormal experience.

The Equipment

First off, this is not going to be a review of every possible piece of equipment one might find in the paranormal investigator's toolbox. It is also not a review of how each piece of equipment works and what it detects. It is assumed that the reader has a good general understanding of the various pieces of equipment that can be used on an investigation, how it works, and what it detects. There are many good books out there that give a complete review of the variety of equipment used by paranormal investigator.

Some important pieces of equipment for detecting and recording changes in environmental conditions associated with hauntings and poltergeists include:

- Electromagnetic and Geomagnetic Field Meters
- Temperature and Humidity Gauges
- Radiation Detectors (Geiger Counters)
- Radio Frequency Meters/Analyzers
- Ion Counters
- Video Recording Systems
- Audio Recording Devices (which will not be covered here since it will be discussed in the chapter on E.V.P.).
- Data Logging Systems such as the S.W.P.R.G.'s *D*irect *E*nvironmental *A*cquisition *D*ata Logging (D.E.A.D.©) System.

Electromagnetic and Geomagnetic Field Meters (EMF and GMF meters)

EMF and GMF meters are by far the most common piece of equipment in the paranormal investigators equipment arsenal. They come in a variety of shapes, sizes, costs, and with different features. Since there are so many different types, there are a few key characteristics that one should know about and look at before deciding to purchase a meter.

- Frequency range. Yes, different meters have different frequency ranges. These range from Extremely Low Frequency (ELF) or Very Low Frequency (VLF) to X-ray to UV. All of these fall within a certain area in the electromagnetic spectrum based on their wavelength and resulting frequency. Therefore, different meters are designed to measure different frequencies. The most common EMF meters are designed to mainly detect changes in the 50/60 hertz mains power frequency. However, it is important to note that they do also pickup frequencies from 30 to 10,000Hz but with different accuracy and frequency weighting (covered more below). Readings are given in milligauss (mG) and/or nanotesla (nT).

- Frequency-weighted meters. Most of the meters out there are frequency-weighted. Why and what does this mean? The body "absorbs' EMFs and the amount of absorption is proportional to the frequency (the higher the frequencies are absorbed more than lower frequencies). Frequency-weighted meters mimic the amount of energy absorbed by the human body. Most meters are calibrated to give an accurate EMF readings at 50/60Hz and then the readings increase based on the frequency detected until it reaches a peak of which then the response drops off. So, if your frequency-weighted meter gives a reading of 10mG for a 50/60Hz field, it means that the field is really 10mG. However, if you are detecting a 100Hz field that theoretically is at 10mG, your meter will give a different reading than 10mG because it is 'interpreting' the frequency as your body would 'see' it as it absorbs that field.
- Non-frequency weighted meters. These meters give a flat response or reading regardless of the frequency. They show the real field strength and not a frequency dependent strength.
- Single-axis meters. These meters only have one sensor to detect the field. In order to get a complete picture of what is going on, one would have to orient the meter and take readings on the X, Y, and Z-axis. Then you would have to calculate the sum using a fancy mathematical equation. The problem with single-axis meters is that something can be easily missed if your meter is not oriented in the same direction that the field is. Also, changes in the orientation of the meter can make you think you have a momentary anomalous reading even though you just simply changed the direction you were holding it.
- 3-axis meters. These meters solve the issues discussed above. They have three sensors with one oriented in each axis—X, Y, and Z. So, you will get an accurate reading no matter what orientation the meter is in. In addition, the meter does the sum calculation for you. Another nice feature, if you want to spend just a little more money, is that you can have the meter display the X, Y, Z-axis individually as well as the SUM! Now that is good information, which will give you a more complete and accurate picture of what is going on with EMFs at haunted locations.

The best way to use these meters on an investigation seems to be to walk a grid pattern. Make sure you walk in the same direction in each room and each time you repeat the measurements (ie: walk from north to south each time). Also, be aware of common sources of spikes and dips such as: clocks, radios, appliances with digital displays, fans, pumps, electric blankets poorly insulated wiring, etc.

Trifield Natural EM Meter

The Trifield Natural EM Meter is one of the most widely recommended and used pieces of equipment within the ghost hunting and paranormal investigation community. The reasons for this are the many unique features that the meter offers:

- It detects extremely weak changes in the static (DC or "natural") electric and magnetic fields.
- It has a magnetic range between 0 to 100 uT (0 to 1000 mG).
- It has a resolution of 2.5 mG in the magnetic range, which is less than 0.5% of the earth's field.
- It is theoretically designed to filter out man-made 50/60 Hz electromagnetic fields.

Because it is designed to filter out man-made 50/60 HZ fields, some people believe that readings on this meter cannot be attributed to manmade sources and therefore must have a paranormal cause. However, a closer look at how this meter functions will provide some food for thought on this issue.

The Trifield Natural EM Meter is calibrated at 2 Hz and it was designed to measure changes down to $\lim(x-0)x$ Hz, which in English means that it measures changes just above 0 Hz but not at 0 Hz [1]. Knowing this, are there manmade fields that could affect this meter? Yes.

In a study done by Schumacher and Carter (2006), it was shown that common household electrical devices and appliances could trigger readings on the Trifield Natural EM Meter. How does this happen? Even though the equipment in the house is at 60 Hz, low frequency fields can be produced in a variety ways by these devices. Where do these fields come from?

One source could be the many transformers and relays in televisions and other household electrical devices. Transformer charging and draining can produce a change in the magnetic field that could be detected by a DC magnetometer or in this case the Trifield Natural EM Meter. Relays contain electromagnets and when power to a device is turned on and flows through the relay this can cause a change in the static field [2].

Changes in the static field could also be produced by turning a 60 Hz electrical device on and off with a somewhat constant frequency. For example, if one turns a hair dryer on and off once every two seconds this would be 'seen' by a DC magnetometer and our Trifield Natural EM Meter as a change in the static field at a frequency of 0.5 Hz (i.e.: one cycle every two seconds).

Also, changes in the amplitude of a 60 Hz signal, with a certain frequency, can be 'seen' by a DC magnetometer and the Trifield Natural EM Meter as changes in the static field [2-3].

There are a variety of other mechanisms and sources that could give rise to low frequency fields in the range that could be detected by this meter. These include:

- The movement or vibration of certain magnetic materials such as iron and steel.
- The motors in furnaces, air-conditioners, washing machines, dryers, and vacuum cleaners. The fields are produced by the magnet in the motor rotating and by the sparking caused by the brushes meeting the commutator.
- Turning various pieces of electrical equipment on and off, which would result in load changes and thereby lead to a change in the main frequency magnetic field.
- Malfunctioning electrical equipment.
- Field leaks from electrical equipment to nearby water pipes [2].

This would indicate that caution should be used before attributing readings on this meter to paranormal activity.

This meter functions by first zeroing out the static field and then measures changes in the field. Therefore, it must remain stationary. Walking around with the meter will do you no good because it will be constantly zeroing out the static field, which could lead to false positive readings.

This meter also has an electric setting in addition to the magnetic setting (and of course there is a sum setting that includes both magnetic and electric). The meter can detect electric fields down to 3 V/m. This is incredibly sensitive and can detect the electric field of the human body. So, no one can be in the room moving around or even in another room close by without tripping the meter. It is best to set the meter somewhere and monitor it remotely using a video surveillance system.

Gaussmeter/Geomagnetometer

These meters also go by the names: Hall-Effect Gaussmeter, DC Magnetometer, and a compass. These meters are designed to detect the earth's magnetic field and therefore are truly calibrated at 0 Hz. They are slightly more expensive, require zeroing and re-zeroing, and a little more complicated to use. But their benefits are certainly worth the time, money, and effort!

Temperature and Humidity Gauges

People have reported drops in temperature before and during paranormal activity. Is it an indicator or effect of paranormal activity? Some people think ghosts draw in thermal energy to manifest. Or could it simply be a draft? What about humidity?

Humidity changes can lead to different 'feelings' in the temperature. How many times does someone refer to a day as being cold and damp?

Besides the 'feelings' associated with humidity, there are physical effects. High levels of humidity can lead to 'fogging' of pictures. Low levels of humidity can lead to higher levels of static electricity, which could:

- Lead to static discharges (shocks) that could interfere with the equipment and could be picked up on photos and/or video or even be seen.
- Lead to lots of static electricity, which could explain that 'charged' and 'energized' environmental feeling that some people report while in a haunted location.
- Give ghosts the energy needed to manifest.

There are two types of devices used by paranormal investigators to detect temperature changes: infrared (IR) thermometer and the digital thermometer/pyrometer.

The infrared thermometer works by projecting an IR beam. When the IR beam hits an object some of the light is reflected and some absorbed by the object. The meter determines the temperature based on the amount of the absorbed and reflected IR light. The IR beam must hit an object with sufficient mass in order to work properly. They don't measure the ambient air temperature.

Now, as said before, we don't know what ghosts are. So, we don't know if they have any mass. Therefore, how do we know that these things are measuring ghostly cold spots and temperature? We don't! There are also other problems using this piece of equipment even if ghosts do have mass and/or they can somehow influence the reading on this thermometer.

There is A LOT of improper use and misinterpretation of the readings obtained. It is common to see people scanning a room and note a 'paranormal' temperature drop. If you look carefully, it turns out that they have aimed it at a window or a cold brick wall or fireplace. It has been said before and it will be said again, BE AWARE OF YOUR SURROUNDINGS!

Using a digital thermometer is the most reliable way to determine the ambient air temperature. These devices are also referred to as thermocouples. The advantage of this over the IR thermometer is that they don't have to come into contact with any type of object with mass in order to get a reading.

The digital pyrometers are more advanced and specialized. They also tend to respond to temperature changes more rapidly. Of course, they cost more!

The above information would indicate that it might be best to use these two different thermometers together to see if they can both detect temperature changes. This would be the best way to cover all your bases until we know what ghosts are or are not.

When using a data logging thermometer, the S.W.P.R.G. has not detected any drops in temperature that could not be explained naturally. However, there have been subjective experiences where S.W.P.R.G. investigators have 'felt' a cold spot or had a cold chill with other environmental changes detected. Let's explore this further by looking at two S.W.P.R.G. case files.

The first example was during an investigation at a private residence in Milwaukee, WI. An S.W.P.R.G. investigator felt a cool breeze down her neck and arm. A photo was taken during this time that showed a dark 'blob' over her head and shoulder. After the feeling had passed, another picture was taken that was normal. Later analysis of the environmental data showed a drop in background radiation levels to 0 cpm only when the experience happened. The levels returned to normal (5 to 10 cpm) once the experience had ended and the normal photo was taken. In addition, during this same time period, there was a shift in the EMF field with a decrease in one axis and an increase in another that correlated perfectly with the investigator's experience and the drop in radiation. There was NO drop in the ambient air temperature recorded on the data logger during this time period.

Another example of experiencing a 'cold spot' / 'cold chill' with no drop in temperature happened during an S.W.P.R.G. investigation of a private residence in Sun Prairie, WI. The investigator walked into an upstairs bedroom and experienced a 'chilled to the bone' feeling. It felt as if the temperature was about 20 degrees colder than the rest of the home and it felt very damp. Another investigator checked the temperature and could not confirm any decrease in the temperature. However, there was a 10-fold increase in the positive ion count (300 ions/cm3 to 3000 ions/cm3) only during the time that the experience happened.

The only thing consistent between these two cases is there was NO decrease in the ambient temperature! So, when one experiences a 'cold spot', perhaps they perceive something else in the environment besides an actual drop in temperature. The brain could be simply perceiving and interpreting some other signal as a drop in the temperature. It would therefore be prudent to measure other things in the environment besides temperature when these 'cold spots' are experienced (such as EMF, ions, radiation, etc.).

Radiation Detectors

Radiation detectors, otherwise commonly known as Geiger Counters, measure the amount of radioactivity in the environment. There are three types of radiation: alpha, beta, and gamma.

Alpha radiation is weak and has very low penetration ability.

Beta radiation is slightly more penetrating than alpha radiation and has a negative charge instead of the associated positive charge that the alpha radiation carries.

Gamma radiation is the best-known form of radiation and is highly penetrating and can be dangerous.

The vast majority of Geiger Counters measure all three forms of radiation and give a sum reading.

So, why would you want to use a Geiger Counter during a paranormal investigation?

The simple answer is that if there is a piece of equipment that measures some kind of background energy (i.e.: radiation) then it is worth using. Especially if one speculates that ghosts manifest using some kind of ambient energy or that ghosts can effect, interact, or change the level of energy in the environment or if changes in environmental energy can affect the living.

The other reason is because parapsychologists and paranormal investigators have previously documented changes in the background radiation levels when a paranormal phenomenon has occurred. Parapsychologists from UCLA used a Geiger Counter during their investigation of the case that was the basis for the movie, *The Entity*. They saw the background radiation levels go down to zero during times of paranormal activity. The readings returned to normal levels when the activity ceased. Other investigators have seen the opposite effect; background levels increase significantly during times of activity and return to normal when the activity ceases.

The S.W.P.R.G. has seen both increases and decreases in the radiation levels that correlated with paranormal activity. These changes also correlated with other environmental changes such as EMFs, E.V.P., picture, ion counts, etc. An example of a decrease in the background levels was mentioned earlier in the Milwaukee, WI case in the temperature section of this chapter. An increase in the background radiation level was documented during an investigation in Watertown, WI. The reading increased approximately 2.5 times the background level only at the exact same time that an E.V.P. was recorded. It then returned to normal when the activity ceased.

It is obvious that the type of change (up or down) in radiation levels during paranormal activity is inconsistent. In addition, there are numerous times when there is paranormal activity and there are no changes in the background radiation levels. Therefore, more data must be collected before any conclusions can be made on whether changes in radiation levels definitely correlate with paranormal activity.

Radio Frequency Meters/Analyzers

Radio frequency (RF) meters/analyzers can tell you what radio frequencies are present in an area and at what strength. There are a variety of different types of these meters available: cell phone detectors, RF Electromagnetic Field Meter, RF Field Strength Analyzer, and Broadcast Frequency Counter to name just a few. They detect frequencies from 100 kHz to 6 GHz with sensitivities of 1 nanoWatt/m2 to 1999 milliWatts/m2 depending on the meter. With all these differences, it is no surprise that the cost will range from $150 to almost $2000.

Now, if you don't want to spend money on another meter and you already have a Trifield Natural EM Meter, you can simply use the radio/microwave setting. It won't tell you the frequency (it picks up frequencies in the range from 100 kHz to 2.5 GHz) but it will give the strength of the signal.

So, what is the purpose of using this kind of equipment during a paranormal investigation? Well, it can be useful for a number of reasons.

First, monitoring for radio frequencies during E.V.P. sessions can help eliminate the possibility that an E.V.P. was just a stray signal from a cell phone, two-way radio, or TV/radio transmission tower. This will help give more credibility to the E.V.P. that you collect.

Second, it will help determine if your own equipment is interfering with your readings (EMF, nEMF, etc). A good example of this is a case the S.W.P.R.G. did in Rockford, IL. At one point we were getting sporadic 10 to 20 mG spikes in the EMF. After a lot of debunking, we discovered that the spikes were due to a cell phone that was not off but on silent and every time a call came in it would cause an EMF spike when the person was relatively close to the equipment. It was also discovered that two-way radios triggered the readings even if they were used in other rooms and on other floors. Testing the area with the RF meter confirmed that the cell phone and two-way radio were the cause of the EMF spikes.

Ion Counters

Ion counters are beginning to become more popular components in the paranormal investigator's toolbox. These devices detect the concentration of positive and negative ions between the ranges of 0 to 1,999,000 ions/cm3.

Ion counters have been used on haunting and poltergeist investigations for a number of years. Excessive positive ion counts (1,500 to greater than 100,000 ions/cm3) have been noted in haunted locations. Relatively high negative ion counts from 3,000 to 8,000 ions/cm3 have also been found in some haunted locations [5].

The S.W.P.R.G. has also noted high positive ion counts in locations with paranormal activity. The occupants generally report a heavy, depressive, sad, or evil feeling in those locations with the high positive ion counts. In contrast, those locations with higher than normal negative ion counts the occupants generally report a benevolent or more positive spirit being present. This correlation is interesting since positive ions have been found to be correlated with irritability and negative moods while negative ions are associated with low irritability and positive moods [6].

This once again leads to the question of a paranormal or normal cause. Is the paranormal activity in the house the cause of the changes in ion levels or do the ion levels have natural sources that cause people to interpret what they are sensing as paranormal? Well, we are not sure what the answer is yet, but we do have evidence of a correlation. In order to understand a possible paranormal cause, all normal explanations must first be understood and explored.

The majority of positive ions come from radioactive decay in the ground, radon in the air, and cosmic rays. Positive ion counts also increase with lightening, before a thunderstorm, high DC voltage (greater than 1000 volts), and vents that are not grounded in cooling systems that use an evaporating water tower. Normal positive ion counts range between 250 to 1,500 ions/cm3.

Positive ions only last about 30 seconds inside to a few minutes outside. This 'life' is determined by how long it takes for the ion to contact something solid (such as dirt or dust) and thereby neutralize the charge. High concentrations of positive ions can attract negative ions so high amounts of both in one area is very possible. Also, high concentrations of just positive ions greater than 100 feet in diameter is very unlikely because they would be unstable and fall apart. Thus, high concentrations of positive ions tend to be rather small and compact.

Negative ions are produced mainly by radioactivity and evaporating water. Negative ion concentrations are known to increase during a thunderstorm, when creating static electricity by combing your hair, and when there is an open flame or an extremely hot object. Normal concentrations of negative ions range between 200 to 800 ions/cm3.

Using the ion counter properly is slightly more complicated than other pieces of equipment. The following pointers will help you get the most accurate readings that you can from your ion counter:

- Make sure the wind guard is properly installed.
- Make sure the ion counter is properly grounded.
- Zero the counter.
- Re-zero the counter every ten minutes and if you change the range setting.
- Wait 10 to 15 seconds before taking a reading when you change the polarity.
- Avoid taking measurements near objects that can hold an excessive charge such as synthetic cloth and plastic objects.
- Make sure that the plastic case has no static charge.
- Be aware that ions may not be uniformly distributed in a location.
- Take numerous readings both in locations where the phenomena was observed to be and where the observer was when they had the experience.
- Try to find normal explanations for high readings (ionizers, air purifiers, fireplaces, furnaces, high static electricity due to low humidity, etc . . .).

- Look for correlations between changes in ion counts and people's subjective paranormal experiences.

Valuable information about the possible correlation between ion counts and paranormal activity can be gained with the ion counter even though it is more complicated to use than other pieces of equipment and there are many things to keep in mind in regards to its proper use.

Fluxgate Magnetometer

This is a relatively new piece of equipment to the paranormal investigation and research community. Dr. Jason Braithwaite and Maurice Townsend from the UK first used it for paranormal research. Recently, the S.W.P.R.G. has been using this equipment on their investigations.

While this meter is expensive ($1,500) and takes some technical skills to use, it is the meter of all meters. Here are a few characteristics that make it unique:

- It is a sensitive high-speed meter.
- It samples AC and DC fields at a high rate on a multi-axis basis.
- It is capable of taking 250 samples per second, which means it can measure frequencies from 0 to 125 Hz.
- It measures the field strength at any given frequency.
- It has a data logging ability.
- Software can be used (i.e.: SigView) to perform FFT analysis. This shows the amplitude at each frequency. It can also determine which frequencies are present.

The extremely precise measurements that this meter can take will allow it to detect large and small changes in the GMF and EMF that may be to rapid and/or small for other meters to detect. Also, knowing what frequencies are present and the amplitudes of each frequency at any given time will help provide a more accurate picture of the role EMFs and GMFs play in paranormal phenomena.

Video Equipment

It's safe to assume that pretty much every group out there has some sort of video system to use on an investigation. So, a few brief comments are warranted.

Different people use a variety of different equipment. This includes everything from VCRs to handycams with nightshot to stand alone DVRs to computer-based systems. However, the main components have stayed the same: a camera, a recording device, and a monitor to watch all the action.

Because there are so many different types of equipment and setups available, the comments here will provide general guidance on what to look for when building your own video monitoring system.

Cameras

Night vision infrared (IR) cameras are the way to go! Now, these are NOT thermal imaging systems that you see on some television shows. These cameras have IR LEDs that illuminate an area with light that can't be seen with the human eye. The camera has the ability to 'see' this light and thus allow you to see in the dark on your video monitor and recording device.

The two main things to look for in a camera are sufficient resolution and IR illumination. The minimum resolution should be 420 lines. In regards to illumination—you'll want to make sure you will be able to illuminate an average size room (10 feet x 10 feet) when it's dark. A minimum of 20 IR LEDs on the camera should do the trick. Now, if you plan on using the cameras in a much bigger room then you should buy a camera with more IR LEDs or you could purchase an IR LED illuminator.

Wireless Transmitters and Receivers for the Cameras

A lot of people detest the thought of running hundreds of feet of cable to hookup their cameras to the recording device so they use wireless transmitters and receivers. After trying these wireless systems, GO WITH THE WIRE! Why? There is endless interference with these systems. Old houses and large buildings have many sources of potential interference. Also, these transmitters can provide another potential source for EMF fluctuations and potential problems during E.V.P. sessions.

Quad Processors

These nifty pieces of equipment allow you to view multiple cameras on one screen, switch between full view screens of each camera, and output the video to a recording device and monitor. They are available in black and white and color displays. Color is the best but if your cameras are only black and white then the additional money for the color model is a waste. Some Digital Video Recorders (DVRs) and computer video interface cards come with quad processors built in. So, if you go that route, don't duplicate your efforts and waste your money on the quad processor.

Recording Devices

Recording devices range from simple self contained handheld video cameras to VCRs to DVD recorders to DVRs to computers. VCRs and DVD recorders can record two to eight hours per tape or disc depending on the model and settings. These are fairly simple to use and require no advance knowledge. DVRs and computers require a little more knowledge and one needs to look for certain specifications when thinking of purchasing this type of equipment.

DVRs and computer video interface cards record video onto a hard drive. Therefore, one needs to consider the level of video quality they want to record and how long they want to record. This will dictate how large the hard drive needs to be. The minimum size of the drive should be 60 GBs.

Another thing to consider when looking at these devices are how many frames per second (fps) they are capable of recording. A minimum of 30 fps per camera is recommended in order to provide smooth quality video. If the DVR or video card interface also has a built in quad processor, then the overall fps must be equal to the number of cameras times 30. For example, if you have 4 cameras then the overall fps would have to be 120 fps (4 cameras x 30 fps per camera = 120 fps).

Finally, since recording time and storage is limited by the size of the hard drive, one will eventually have to transfer the video to a tape or disk in order to have a permanent recording for the case file. This is easily done using a VCR or DVD recorder.

Motion Detection Recording

Watching hours upon hours of video can be tedious and boring. If you record eight hours of video on four different cameras this would mean you have to review 32 hours of video! YIKES! In order to reduce the amount of video to watch some people have begun to experiment with motion detection recording. Video is only recorded when motion is detected.

Motion detection is accomplished in one of two ways. The first being the camera itself has a Passive Infrared (PIR) sensor that works the same way as the common IR motion detector. When the PIR sensor detects a rapid change in motion and temperature (i.e.: the IR energy it is 'seeing') it sends a signal back to the receiving unit that then triggers the recording device to begin recording.

This seems like a good idea to only record motion when the PIR sensor is triggered. However, it is possible that it will miss something paranormal. We don't know what ghosts are and therefore we don't know if they would be able to trigger the PIR sensor. So, it is feasible that one may miss something important because it simply didn't trigger the sensor.

The second method of motion detection is the computer program or DVR begins recording based on motion detection through pixel changes. The sensitivity and area for motion detection is adjustable. This may be a better choice since it simply detects motion by changes in the image and does not need anything to trigger an external sensor such as the PIR sensor.

The main problem with both of these methods is what if the ghost does not affect the camera? What if the ghost uses PK to manipulate the recording media directly? This is certainly possible since parapsychological researchers have documented people being able to imprint images onto undeveloped film. It would be interesting to run both types of systems to see what would happen.

Direct Environmental Acquisition Data logging (D.E.A.D.©) System

The D.E.A.D.© system consists of the following:

- Triaxial ELF magnetic field meter with pc interface. The meter has a bandwidth of 30Hz to 2000Hz and an accuracy of +/-3% at 50Hz/60Hz and +/-5% at 40 to 200Hz. Data is logged using the supplied software.
- HOBO Temperature data logger from Onset Computer Corporation with data logging and archiving ability. Software provided by Onset Computer Corporation is used for data logging and archiving.
- GM-10 radiation detector from Black Cat Systems with pc interface. The Radiation Acquisition and Display (RAD) software is used to log and archive the data. Radiation detected includes alpha, beta, and gamma/x-ray. Data is displayed as counts per minute (cpm).
- Panasonic Toughbook CF-45 laptop computer.
- Tri-field natural EMF meter modified to be data logged by the HOBO data logger.
- Fluxgate Magnetometer Model 539 with APS software. Set to collect approximately 400 samples per second. Data is analyzed using SigView.

The S.W.P.R.G. designed and developed the *Direct Environmental Acquisition Data* logging (D.E.A.D.©) system in order to data log and analyze large amounts of environmental data during investigations. Data logging with date-time stamping allows us to look for correlations between the different environmental changes, subjective paranormal experiences, and anomalies on video and in photographs. Being able to correlate at least two pieces of data (i.e.: EMF and a personal experience, radiation drops and an anomaly on a photo, radiation spike and a recorded E.V.P., etc) provides more credible evidence AND allows us to discover what the correlations might be between paranormal phenomena and environmental changes. Ultimately, this type of quality information may help us determine how a haunting affects the environment, what is normal and what is paranormal, if environmental changes cause people to have subjective paranormal experiences, and what type of information is needed to determine what a haunting is and is not. This is the type of information that is needed in order to advance the field of paranormal investigation.

How is the D.E.A.D.© system unique?

While the idea of a data logging system is not new (others include: MESA, GEIST, ARCADIA, and MADS), this system is especially unique in the type and quality of the data collected, especially for EMFs.

- The Triaxial ELF magnetic field meter records data independently on the X, Y, and Z-axes every 1 sec. A SUM measurement is also recorded. The resulting data can then be analyzed and graphed using any number of software programs.
- The fluxgate magnetometer model 539 is an extremely sensitive high-speed sensor that offers many unique features that are useful for paranormal work: it samples AC and DC fields at a high rate on a multi-axis basis (X, Y, Z and SUM); it has a fast sample rate of at least 250 samples per second; it measures field strength; it can measure changes down to 0.005mG; and it measures the field strength at any given frequency. Not only can we determine changes in the field BUT we can also determine the frequency!

Why is the D.E.A.D.© system essential to what we do?

- Meters that report only the SUM may not provide the entire story of what is happening with the spatial and temporal changes in the EMFs. For example, if there was a 4mG drop in the X-axis with a corresponding 4mG increase in the Y-axis, the SUM may only show a small change if it would show one at all. Therefore, recording data independently for the X, Y, and Z-axes in addition to the SUM will provide greater insight as to what is happening with the EMFs.
- Data logging is essential if we are to determine if subjective paranormal experiences coincide with environmental changes. Other investigators have reported changes such as temperature drops, EMF spikes, motion detectors going off, etc during a paranormal experience. On the other hand, people have reported experiences with no equipment readings. So, what is really happening? Perhaps the equipment used was not sensitive enough. Maybe there was a change in one axis while there was an opposite change in another axis and it was not detected in the SUM reading. The investigator using handheld equipment may have simply missed the reading due to the excitement felt during the experience. It is also possible that the entire experience was in the head of the investigator and there was no environmental change at all. Using a highly accurate data logging system helps alleviate some of these possible problems and assist in elucidating what is really happening.

The following are examples of some of the data the D.E.A.D.© system can collect and its' usefulness.

The first one is from a case at a private home in Milwaukee.

- At approximately 7:50pm, an investigator reported feeling a cold 'draft/breeze' around her neck/should/arm area.
- Another investigator took a time series of photos during this experience.
- The photo at 7:50pm shows a dark mass/shadow/blob over the investigator's head.
- (Pic #1)
- The radiation also drops to 0 cpm. (Radiation Chart)
- There was a drop in Y-axis EMF and an increase in the Z-axis EMF. (Not Shown)
- Another photo taken a few seconds later shows nothing. (Not Shown)
- Another photo taken at 7:53pm also shows nothing. (Not Shown)
- There was no decrease in temperature recorded during this time period.

(Pic #1)   (Pic #2)

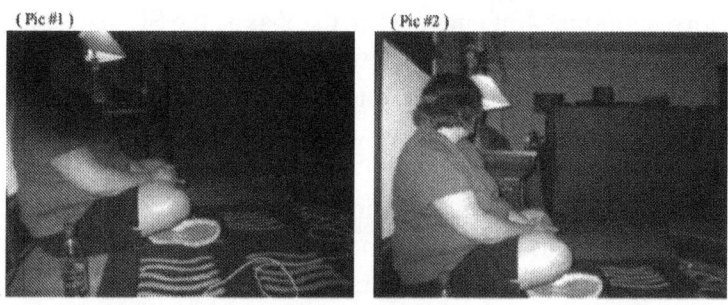

(Radiation Chart 1)

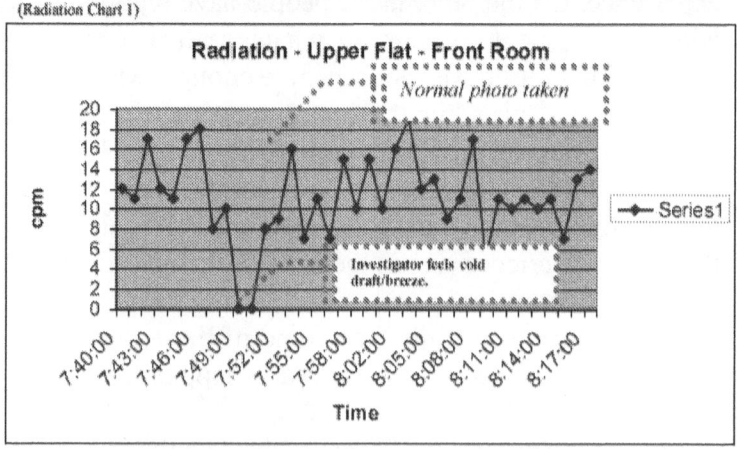

Here is another example of EMF data that was collected when people were having auditory experiences at a private home in Sun Prairie, WI.

1. The owner and a S.W.P.R.G. investigator were in the small upstairs bedroom, referred to as the Children's Room, when they both heard someone say, "Hey."
2. Two investigators asked, "Can you show yourself to us?" A voice saying, "Yes" was heard by the investigators who were the only people in the room at that time.
3. A whimpering sound was heard by three of the six people in the room.
4. There was a large 'spike' in the EMF of 267mG when the owner attempted to antagonize whatever was there.

The graph below shows the EMF data collected during the times that the above events occurred. The numbers above the 'spikes' on the graph correlate with the numbered events above.

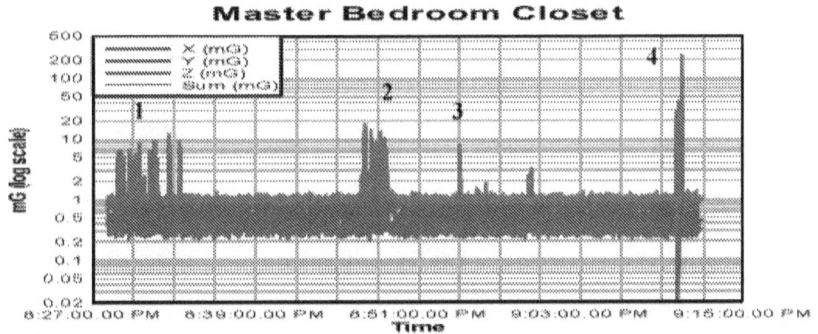

As one can see, data logging with the D.E.A.D.© system provides an incredible amount of accurate and correlated data.

Chapter 7

ELECTROMAGNETIC FIELDS
WHY ARE WE SO ATTRACTED TO THEM?

One of the most common pieces of technological equipment in the ghost hunter's and paranormal investigator's arsenal is the electromagnetic field (EMF) meter. This includes 60Hz EMF meters, Tri-Field meters, triaxial EMF meters, natural EMF meters, and geomagnetic field (GMF) meters.

The question is: why do we use them? Investigators give various reasons when asked this question and a few of the more common responses are listed below:

1. They detect ghosts
2. Ghosts are made of EMFs
3. Ghosts alter the EMFs when they manifest
4. Ghosts use EMFs as an energy source to manifest
5. Ghosts emit EMFs
6. The more scientifically savvy investigators point to the work and theories of Professor McFadden of the School of Biomedical and Life Sciences at the University of Surrey in the UK. Professor McFadden believes that consciousness is an electromagnetic field. His research has shown that when a neuron fires, that 'piece of electrical information' becomes part of or 'bound' together with all the other signals in the brain in its electromagnetic field. Some ghost hunters and paranormal investigators believe that the brain's electromagnetic field (consciousness) would be the only thing that survives bodily death, based on the first law of thermodynamics.

However, this has never been proven and many other scientists have certainly challenged Professor McFadden's theory.

7. And then there is our all time favorite-because everybody else does it!

The main problem with all of these reasons is that there isn't any good evidence to support them. So, why should we continue to measure EMFs? What do we really know about EMFss/GMFs and ghostly phenomena? *Why should we continue to monitor them?*

1. We must collect data to see if there is a correlation between EMFs/GMFs and paranormal activity.
2. We just don't know what ghosts are or how they manifest. Could they use EMFs/GMFs to manifest? Possibly. Do ghosts emit EMFs/GMFs? Are they made of EMFs/GMFs? Do they alter EMFs/GMFs? Since we don't know what ghosts are, there is no way we know the answers to these questions.
3. Scientific research has shown that EMFs/GMFs can stimulate brain activity (cause hallucinations, sense of presence, and trigger seizures in epileptics) and that haunted locations may have magnetically distinct signatures. Let's take a closer look at this information.

It has been known for some time that EMFs and GMFs (especially those in the low frequency range of 0.5Hz to 40Hz) can induce neurophysiological activity and experiential changes in people [1-11]. Increases in geomagnetic activity have been found to trigger seizures in people with complex partial epilepsy [38]. On the paranormal side, increases in geomagnetic activity have been found to correlate with an increase in apparitional sightings, bereavement apparitions, and poltergeist activity [5, 11, 12, 39]. With this information, scientists began lab experiments with EMFs to see if they could induce/create haunting-like experiences.

A variety of experiments have been done which involve applying EMFs to the heads of test subjects and then asking them what they experience and/or measuring brain wave patterns with EEG. Earlier experiments used surgical stimulation of the temporal lobes, which resulted in the feeling of a sensed presence [40]. More recent experiments involved applying complex transcerebral frequency-modulated-magnetic fields to the heads of test subjects [10-12, 41-43]. Subjects reported a variety of experiences, including: feelings of a sensed presence, having an apparitional experience, shadows moving around, someone touching their left side, a foreboding feeling, flashes of light, shivers, involuntary movement, and feelings of being controlled [10-12, 41-42]. One experiment even found that the effect of "weak complex magnetic fields, can be encouraged by increased geomagnetic activity" [41].

With this information, along with various other studies, researchers suggested that EMFs and/or GMFs could be responsible for 'haunt-type' experiences [11-12] and may be present at locations that have produced multiple instances of spontaneous paranormal experiences [10, 12-15]. So . . . . they went ghost hunting!

The researchers wanted answers to the following questions: Do haunted locations have differences in their EMFs/GMFs compared to locations that are not haunted? How are the EMFs/GMFs different? Are they elevated? Are they frequency modulated? Are they simple or complex fields? Are there spatial and temporal variations even within a haunted location? The following points below are a summary of the major findings from various studies.

- Haunted locations have increased levels of ambient spatially specific EMFs and/or GMFs [11-15, 18-21].
- Some researchers found that there was nothing special about the background fields but there were significant pulses and/or variability [22-24].
- Increases in the GMF between 20nT to 50nT are associated with haunt-type experiences and reports of a 'sensed presence' [10, 14].

Very detailed studies of EMFs at Muncaster castle found:

- Locations where people have had spontaneous paranormal experiences have magnetically remarkable signatures.
- Magnetic anomalies exist at locations of interest and specific areas within those locations.
- The amplitudes of the fields are spatially and temporally complex and variable.
- The predominant frequency was 50Hz (the AC field in the UK).
- There were inverted pulses in the AC field with a duration of 480ms. The pulse depth was 11nT to 31nT and the peak amplitude was 7nT to 49nT.
- Pulses were at intervals of multiples of eight seconds: eight seconds (0.125Hz), 16 seconds (0.0625Hz), 24 seconds (0.042Hz), and 32 seconds (0.031Hz).

- The authors commented that even though the pulses are from a 50Hz field, it would be 'seen' by a DC magnetometer and a human brain as a pulse in the static field [25-26].

Investigators with the Southern Wisconsin Paranormal Research Group (S.W.P.R.G.) using the *D*irect *E*nvironmental *A*cquisition *D*ata logging (D.E.A.D.©) system have seen similar characteristics in the EMFs at haunted locations. Three examples are shown below (two haunted locations and one with no history of paranormal activity).

- **The Rockford Register Star**
The EMF levels on the fifth floor ranged between .956mG to 5.936mG. Pulses were seen between 3mG to 5mG (300nT to 500nT). The pulses occurred once every 4, 8, 18, 26, 28, 30, 32, or 34 seconds (0.25Hz, 0.125Hz, 0.05Hz, 0.04Hz, 0.036Hz, 0.033Hz, 0.030Hz, and .029Hz).
- **The Octagon House**
There were pulses in the EMF every 6 to 8 seconds. These pulses are interesting because of their low frequency (0.125Hz to 0.16Hz) and amplitude (approximately .3mG or 30nT).

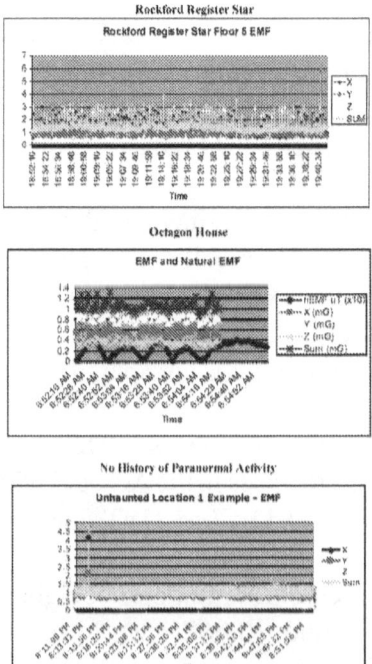

Therefore, it seems as if the complexity of the magnetic field is important and not just the overall amplitude [10, 12-17, 22-26].

So, where does this leave us?

Some propose a very natural explanation. Exposure to such fields could cause observers to bias their impressions of ambiguous stimuli towards a paranormal interpretation within a certain 'magnetic complex' [10, 26, 28-30].

However, this still doesn't explain the accurate and repeatable historical context reported by different people with no knowledge of the area/situation. What other possible explanations could there be?

Let's look at this information within the context of the five hypotheses that were presented in chapter 5. Here is a review of those hypotheses:

1. The Neurological Hypothesis. Exposure to certain environmental factors or energies or certain frequencies can affect the brain, which in turn can cause a person to hallucinate.
2. The Perceptual Hypothesis. Exposure to certain environmental energies affects brain functioning, which allows one to perceive unusual events or objects, like ghosts that we can't perceive in ordinary states of consciousness. This is also known as Budden's Electro-Staging Hypothesis. Budden feels that these energies unleash the power of the unconscious, which leads to 'staged' hallucinatory experiences. This would also somewhat fit in with Tyrell's 'idea-pattern' theory of telepathically induced hallucinations. However, Budden does not discuss telepathy. This is covered in the telepathic hypothesis.
3. The Telepathic Hypothesis. Telepathy affects brain functioning, causing the telepathic communication to be perceived as if it were projected from outside the body.
4. Psychokinetic Hypothesis. Intense subjective experiences intrude on the physical world.
5. The Ghost Hypothesis. Apparitions are genuine, independent entities that can be directly perceived or independently detected as anomalous energetic effects.

There could also be a combination of any of the above hypotheses. [31-35]. Which hypothesis is correct? It seems as if the evidence points to number one if you don't think there is anything paranormal going on. On the other hand, if there is some sort of paranormal activity then perhaps numbers two, four, or five (that is if ghosts somehow affect the magnetic fields). However, hypothesis three is still a possibility especially if one considers that some researchers have failed to find any magnetically distinguishing features between haunted and non-haunted areas in locations of interest [36-37].

What are the implications of this information for paranormal investigators and the use of EMF/GMF monitoring equipment?

1. Continue to monitor, collect, and data log EMF and GMF data.
2. Data logging is the preferred method of data collection due to temporal and spatial variability and the 'spikes' and 'dips' in data over time.
3. EMF and GMF data should be collected from 'haunted' locations in the following areas: where the person was at time of perception of the phenomena, where the phenomena were perceived to be, and locations where there has been NO reported phenomena. This will help determine if there are 'magnetic signatures' in areas where phenomena are reported.
4. Do not dismiss high ambient background EMF and GMF readings (even if they are due to man-made sources . . . ie: AC). Monitor these locations and those nearby for temporal and spatial variations. Also, monitor for 'spikes' and 'drops' in those locations.
5. Consider the purchase and use of more sensitive monitoring equipment such as that used in some of the studies referenced above [25-26].

Chapter 8

E.V.P.: AN OVERVIEW
by Cindy Heinen

Voice recorders are a mainstay item in a paranormal investigator's toolbox. Cassette, digital or a computer recording system are all used in the hopes of collecting E.V.P. E.V.P., electronic voice phenomena, is the capturing of paranormal sounds and voices on a recording device.

History of E.V.P.

Since the invention of recording devices, there has been documentation of individuals having paranormal experiences while using communication and recording equipment. Stories have been reported of paranormal messages coming through wireless Morse code systems. Children's author Grace Duffie Boylan wrote the 1918 book, Thy Son Liveth: Messages From a Soldier to His Mother. The book documents Mrs. Boylan's contacts with her dead son. The first of these contacts was through Morse code messages she claims her son sent after he was killed during a battle in WWI [4].

In 1877, Thomas Alva Edison's words, "Mary had a little lamb," were the first recorded onto a tinfoil cylinder phonograph. This event ushered in the development of recording machines [30]. It appears Edison, in his later years, had an interest in developing a device that could be used to communicate with the personalities of the deceased. Although writings remain that indicate his interest in doing this, no actual schematics for such a machine or the device itself have been found [2].

In the 1920's through the 1950's a handful of inventors and people interested in spirit communication attempted to find a technological connection to the spirit word. Some individuals attempted to record direct spirit voices that were produced during séances. Others became interested in the recording of spirit voices after unintentionally recording voices of people they knew to be deceased.

"Of course I'll help you," were the first words heard during the playback of a wired magnetophone being used by Father Marcello Pellegrino Ernetti and Father Agostin Gemelli to record Gregorian chants in Italy in 1952. This came as a shock to both men, but especially to Father Gemelli, as he recognized the voice as his deceased father. The voice seemed to be in reply to an exasperated Father Gemelli's plea for help from his late father in the fixing of a broken wire on the magnetophone. The two priests were later able to obtain additional voices from Father Gemelli's father [20].

In the 1950's Attila von Szalay, a photographer and medium, teamed up with researcher and author Raymond Bayless in a series of controlled experiments. In 1959 they published an article about their experiments in the Journal of the American Society for Psychical Research. For these experiments Szalay was put in a cabinet that contained a microphone placed in a speaking trumpet. These long, cone shaped trumpets were often used by mediums to assist in the manifestation of direct spirit voices during séances. The microphone was connected to a tape recorder and a loudspeaker that were placed outside of the cabinet. Using this system they were able to capture and document voices of people they believed to be dead [16].

But it was the dedicated research of Friedrich Juergenson that brought recorded spirit communication into the public eye. Health related issues had brought Juergenson's career as an opera singer to a halt, just two years after going professional. Fortunately, he had also trained as a painter and easily slipped into this profession. His talents as a painter led to a life of travel and exhibitions. It was in 1958 after he had completed an exhibit of his painting in Pompeii that Friedrich Juergenson's life was to be changed forever.

He and his wife had decided to travel to their property in the country for a weekend holiday. Juergenson had brought along his reel-to-reel tape recorder in hopes of recording the songs of the many birds that filled the springtime countryside. In the attic of his forest hut around four o'clock on Friday, June 12, 1959, he placed a microphone from the recorder close to an open window and turned on the recorder in hopes of recording the song of a finch that was near the house. Upon playback of this five-minute recording, he was disappointed to find that the finches' song was almost completely covered by a hissing, static sound. Although he suspected a damaged tube was the culprit of this distortion, he tried another recording. As he played back this second recording he heard the same hissing sound, but suddenly out of the hissing came the sound of a trumpet followed by the very quiet sound of a man talking about the bird songs of the night, complete with the sound of chirping birds. Suddenly these birds and the hissing sound vanished and were replaced by the song of the finch he had attempted to originally record [15].

Juergenson was a man of intellect and questioned this strange event. He considered the possibility of radio interference, but because of his isolated location far from other radios, he felt this was unlikely.

Although he tried, Juergenson did not receive a similar recording until a month later on July 12. In the series of voices recorded that evening he was personally addressed by a voice stating, "Friedrich, you're being observed" [15].

Juergenson, who died in 1987, spent the rest of his life recording and cataloging the voices of what he finally came to believe were from the dead. He wrote books on the subject and was the subject of numerous magazine and newspaper articles. Many, who were interested in the taped voice phenomena, including Dr. Konstantine Raudive, sought him out.

Raudive had become interested in Juergenson's work, and after visiting him, decided to start his own research. From 1965 until his death, it is claimed he compiled hundreds of thousands of paranormal voices on tape. Many of these voices spoke in multilingual sentences. It is not uncommon to see a translation of a Raudive recording that lists the languages of Russian, Italian and English within a single E.V.P. phrase. This fact has put Raudive's work under scrutiny and he was accused of being uncritical and unyielding in his interpretations of the voices he recorded.

Raudive was the author of the book, *Breakthrough, The Inaudible Becomes Audible.* This extensive book and its accompanying 33 1/3 RPM record of voice examples, documented Raudive's experiences in what had by then been coined Electronic Voice Phenomena or E.V.P.

Other individuals followed and became devoted experimenters in E.V.P. Raymond Cass of England, Sarah Estep of the United States, and Marcelo Bacci of Italy are just a few of the dedicated researchers who have devoted much of their lives to the recording and studying of E.V.P.

Characteristics

E.V.P. is a part of Instrumental Transcommunication (ITC). ITC is the capturing of what is thought to be spirit communications through electronic devices. These communications can be visual through techniques that utilize video cameras, televisions and monitors, or can be written communications found in computer files or faxes. There are even claims of two way, real time communication between ethereal beings and experimenters that happen via radio and telephone. E.V.P., which is the audio aspect of ITC, is generally not heard at the time of recording, but is found during the playback of the recording device. In addition to this characteristic, experimenters have discovered some other commonalities about E.V.P.

First, the E.V.P. utterances are short in duration, usually only one to three seconds in length. The words are usually spoken very quickly but are complete, meaning they do not start in mid-syllable, but it is not uncommon for longer phrases to fade out towards the end.

Although E.V.P. can be isolated utterances, they can also come in layers with voices overlapping one another. Another characteristic is that individual utterances can be linked to one another and separated by a short pause. Alexander MacRae of Scotland has made a study of this and has theorized that E.V.P. utterances are limited by available energy. This pause may be an attempt to utilize this available energy to create a burst of communication [7].

The quality of E.V.P. utterances has been found to have variations. The utterances can be whispers, have a harsh static sound, sound mechanical or monotone, or take on the characteristics of whatever sounds are in the environment's background noise. The voices can also have a lyric, song-like quality or sound very close to a normal human voice.

When the voices are clear, one can sometime recognize the gender and age of the speaker. Emotions can be heard in some voices. Individuals have claimed to recognize certain voices as someone they knew in life. This can be based on recognizing the sound of the voice as well as idiosyncrasy in the use of words or phrases unique to the deceased person.

Since the clarity and quality of E.V.P. varies greatly, a grading system was developed by United States E.V.P. pioneer Sarah Estep. E.V.P. are graded on an A, B, and C scale. A class A E.V.P. voice is clearly heard and understood by most people, even through loud speakers. A class B E.V.P., although not as clear or loud as a class A, can still be understood by most people but a slight difference of interpretation might arise. Class B are best listened to through headphones. Class C E.V.P. are usually found deep in background noise. They must be listened to with headphones and interpretations may be questioned [11].

Although clear, some E.V.P. utterances just seem nonsensical. English E.V.P. researcher Judith Chisholm has noted from the many E.V.P. she has analyzed that some have "disregard for the laws of grammar" [9].

George Gilbert Bonner, a UK psychotherapist who started researching E.V.P. in 1972, noted that even though he recorded sentences of normal length, few continued on to a conversation [9].

For example many E.V.P. investigators have received the utterance, "Help me," only to never receive any follow up voice to indicate how they could help.

Numerous investigators have captured E.V.P. voices that indicate interaction between the investigator and the E.V.P. speaker. These interactions may be the direct answering of a question during an E.V.P. session or a comment about what investigators are doing. These E.V.P. comments are not uncommon and are often quite clear. The Southern Wisconsin Paranormal Research Group (S.W.P.R.G.) has encountered E.V.P. of this nature on investigations. An E.V.P. of exceptional quality occurred during the equipment tear down at the end of a Wisconsin investigation. A whispered voice is interjected twice into the investigators conversation about breaking down the equipment. The E.V.P. can be heard on: *http://www.paranormalresearchgroup.com/EVP.html*

This is only a short list of E.V.P. characteristics and common occurrences that many E.V.P. investigators share. It shows the wide realm that E.V.P. can encompass.

What Is or Isn't E.V.P.?

One of the puzzles early researchers tried to solve was who or what was producing the voices. Juergenson originally believed the voices were produce by other worldly beings or extraterrestrials [15]. Early in his E.V.P. research, he changed to believing that the voices were those of the deceased. He also documented receiving a handful of voices that were those of people he knew not to be deceased [15].

Other researchers have also attributed the voices to multiple sources. Sarah Estep, who attributed many voices to deceased people, also recorded the voices of those she believed to be from outer space [11].

The husband and wife team of Maggy Harsch-Fischbach and Jules Harsch made recordings of their contact with what they contended was a team of spiritual beings from a group named Timestream. This team, which was said to consist of both deceased individuals and other world beings, was to assist the couple in improving contact [17]. Other researchers claim to have made contact with Timestream or other similar helper groups.

These claims suggest that there may be multiple sources of E.V.P. The most common source experienced by investigators is an E.V.P. produced by a discarnate being or ghost. Whether this spirit is connected to the location of the investigation, connected to someone in the group, or just "playing through" can sometimes be discerned from the E.V.P. message itself.

Residual energy or a residual haunting may account for some E.V.P. Examples of this are E.V.P. captured from battlefields. Recordings from Gettysburg and other famous battlefields sometimes contain the sounds of gun and cannon fire, horses, and the sounds of commands being given. These E.V.P. might just be the playback of these horrific events or the spontaneous discharge of some type of residual energy.

As stated earlier, Friedrich Juergenson claimed to have picked up the voices of people he knew not to be dead. His experience, along with similar experiences of other researchers, may indicate that living people have the ability to produce voices on recording devices through psychokinesis. Parapsychologist Loyd Auerbach defines psychokinesis, or PK, as "the ability of the mind to influence objects or processes without the use of a known physical process" [1]. PK can come in different forms from the ability to move objects with one's mind to the studied ability of Ted Serios who could "think" images onto camera film [10]. It is thought that a similar PK effect could result in the formation of E.V.P. voices on a recorder.

Voices produced by other-world beings, although intriguing, may be the hardest to verify. Those who claim to have captured these voices usually come to this conclusion based on what the message says, sometimes coupled with unusual phenomena that may follow or coincide with the voice.

But not every unexplained sound or static interference found on a recorder is an E.V.P. To analyze E.V.P. one must be grounded in what physical and environmental factors could produce sounds that could easily be mistaken for E.V.P. Many of these same factors are the evidence put forth by skeptics and debunkers to disprove all E.V.P. A thorough investigator shouldn't be put off by this and should instead take a serious look at each of these factors when analyzing suspected E.V.P. voices.

Stray radio, television, CB transmissions and cell phone waves are just few of the thousands of electromagnetic waves that permeate the atmosphere. Cross-modulation, or the picking up of these waves on recording devices, can happen. Many people who record E.V.P. are often affronted when this idea is suggested. Although it may be a rare occurrence, it has been the author's personal experience of picking AM radio stations during recording sessions, which proves that this event can happen. Several precautions can be taken to reduce the possibility of this happening. The first would be to provide a shielded environment, not only for recorders, but also for microphones. An external microphone cable can act as an antenna and pick up both radio and electrical equipment interference. Using a shielded microphone cable is one precaution an experimenter can take. Also, be aware of the recording location. Look for cell phone towers and broadcasting transmitters. During analysis, recordings that pick up long segments of dialogue and music need to be scrutinized. Remember that most E.V.P. are short, only 1 to 3 seconds long and anything else needs to be looked at carefully.

Misinterpreting sounds as E.V.P. voices is a type of pareidolia. Robert Carroll's website, *The Skeptic's Dictionary*, defines pareidolia as "a type of illusion or misperception involving a vague or obscure stimulus being perceived as something clear and distinct" [8]. We naturally look for patterns in visual and auditory information. In the case of E.V.P. this would mean finding speech patterns in random noise. This most commonly would happen when working with class C E.V.P. It's easier to do then one may believe, especially with digital recorders that can distort the tonal quality or timbre of sounds. Using a background noise source, especially a loud one, can also mask and distort everyday sounds.

Audio fatigue can result in mistaking sounds for paranormal voices. Listening intently to recordings for long periods of time, especially those from an internally noisy recorder can desensitize the ears. Prolonged, intent listening also has the potential for harming one's hearing. The inner ear's cochlea has up to 30,000 hair cells that will react to sound and stimulate the auditory nerve system [14]. These hair cells will become taller in very quiet environments and get shorter in noisy environments. If there is too much noise or prolonged exposure to noise these hair cells will not react as efficiently and the listener, in addition to auditory fatigue, could experience tinnitus, a ringing or buzzing in the ears. Over exposure to noise can also result in a condition called temporary threshold shift, in which muffled speech and even the symptoms of tinnitus will last for an extended period of time [24]. Listening for E.V.P. utterances may not be the same as listening to loud music, but during analysis, the use of headphones can increase the playback volume to an unsafe decibel level. The best defense against mistaking noise for voices and against damaging hearing is to take frequent breaks during analysis and keep the headphone volume at a safe level.

Factors That May Contribute to the Capture of E.V.P.

Defining who or what is making E.V.P. voices, be it normal or paranormal, isn't the only challenge facing E.V.P. investigators. Another puzzle E.V.P. investigators continually struggle with is how to improve the quality and the quantity of the voices. What factors contribute to successful E.V.P. collection, and can these factors be duplicated so anyone can get the same results?

There are at least four factors that may influence the collection of E.V.P. They are the human factor, location, environmental factors and equipment used.

Many E.V.P. researchers claim the human factor is the most important in obtaining E.V.P. The investigator may be an integral part in the process of collecting an E.V.P. It has been suggested that intent, interest, energy level, consistency of recording, and even the investigator's mediumistic or psychic ability can play a part in the collection of E.V.P. [7].

William O'Neil, for example, was said to be a gifted medium and was also the only person who could reliably get George Meek's Spiricom device to work. Spiricom (Mark I through V) was a communication device that included a set of 13 tone generators spanning the range of an adult male's voice. O'Neil was reported to have had real time conversations with, among others, a deceased NASA physicist who helped him with improvements to Spiricom [18].

Included in the human factor is what appears to be a learning curve in one's ability to collect E.V.P. While some investigators are able to start obtaining E.V.P. utterances from their first recording, most people seem to have to make several attempts before getting a first voice.

It is said you can record any place and capture E.V.P. Field investigators record E.V.P. in locations that are claimed to experience paranormal activity. This could be any location from a house or business to a cemetery. And while recording in such an active location should result in capturing E.V.P., this is not always the case. There are other researchers who record in one set location. This location will often be a room in the researcher's home that usually was never linked to paranormal activity. Individuals who record in set location seem to take longer to get a first E.V.P. than field investigators who record in a variety of haunted locations. World ITC director Mark Macy wrote that it took four months of persistent recording sessions from his living room until he received his first E.V.P. [19]. But it seems contacts that are eventually made in set locations more frequently respond to direct questions. Another interesting phenomenon is that these researchers report capturing E.V.P. from the same spirits repeatedly. At times these E.V.P. are recognized as deceased family members. It has been suggested that it is possible to build up a positive field of energy in a set location that might assist with recording these E.V.P. [7].

Environmental factors, such as those that apply to general paranormal investigations, may assist E.V.P. pickup. These are weather, moon phases, solar flare activity, geomagnetic activity and Local Sidereal Time. Anecdotal evidence seems to indicate that more E.V.P. can be captured at night or during stormy weather then during the day or in clear weather. Although many investigators get E.V.P. during the day and in clear weather, the apparent increase in activity during the night and stormy weather could indicate an atmospheric condition that is better suited for E.V.P. collection. Friedrich Juergenson claimed he obtained his best recordings during the summer months after sunset and during dry, cold weather in winter before sunset [9].

It is common practice in the ghost hunting community to check solar flare and geomagnetic activity before an investigation. Many paranormal groups feel that activity in these two events will result in an increase in haunting activity. Does this also affect the quality and quantity of E.V.P. voices an investigator can expect to get? In a study done by the Southern Wisconsin Paranormal Research Group, three data sets of E.V.P. collected from three different sources between 2001 and 2005 were examined. These E.V.P. were analyzed to determine if there was a correlation between an increase in the geomagnetic field and the quantity of E.V.P. The results of this study showed no such correlation [31]. Nevertheless, sometimes an increased in the electromagnetic field (EMF) is noted just before or during an E.V.P. utterance. More study will be needed in this area.

Scientist James Spottiswoode has conducted research that looked at environmental conditions and the psychic or psi ability of test subjects. In one particular study he looked at psi test results and how they corresponded to sidereal time. Local Sidereal Time (LST) can be considered star time and differs from solar time. A solar day is the time from when the sun is in any given location in the sky to the next time the sun is in that location. A sidereal day is the time from when the stars are in any given location to the next time that they are in that location. A sidereal day is approximately four minutes shorter then a solar day. Dr. Spottiswoode found that during a particular window of time, 13:30 h LST, the psi ability of the test subjects increased dramatically [32]. Other researchers have found similar results. Dr. Rupert Sheldrake and Pamela Smart noted in a study that analyzed a dog's apparent telepathic bond with its owner that the results seemed to be significantly affected by LST [26]. Some in the E.V.P. community suggest that consideration of LST could positively affect the outcome of E.V.P. sessions.

The Anomalous Research Department of the S.W.P.R.G. conducted a pilot study that looked at the number of E.V.P. collected at 13:50 LST, the time shown in prior studies to show the highest increase psi ability, and 18:00 LST, the time shown in prior studies to have the greatest negative effect on psi ability. The results of this study showed no affect or correlation between the 13:50 LST window and E.V.P. [13].

Equipment may seem to be the only controllable factor in E.V.P. investigation. Can specialized equipment increase the amount and quality of E.V.P. voices? Certainly the equipment we use today is far more sophisticated than equipment early researchers used, but are the results any better? The basic equipment used during investigations includes cassette recorders, digital recorders, and computers using recording programs. Juergenson and other early researchers used vacuum tube, reel-to-reel tape recorders. In the sixties the Dutch company Philips invented the compact audio cassette [12]. One of the first cassette player/recorders was the Norelco Carry-Corder 150 [30]. The small, portable size of the cassette player and the reusable, snap-in cassette cartridges were features that made this format highly successful in the private market. For the general public, the cassette eventually replaced the reel-to-reel recorder. E.V.P. investigators also found the cassette recorders a convenient tool.

In the 1980's and 90's a whirlwind of development in integrated circuits (IC) was the impetus for the production of a new generation of personal electronic devices. For the paranormal researcher the IC recorder, more commonly called a digital note-taker, started to replace magnetic tape recorders as the recorder of choice for E.V.P. The note-taker's tiny size and ease of use added to its attractiveness as an investigative recorder, but a key reason for its soaring popularity seemed to be its superior ability to pick up E.V.P.

One reason why these recorders seem conducive to picking up E.V.P. may lie in the electrical circuits. One hypothesis is that the poor quality sound circuits, especially in early models, tend to produce internal noise. It is suggested that this internal noise may act as a carrier wave for a spirit to use to generate a voice. That a spirit needs a background noise source to be able to produce an audible voice on tape is the belief of many E.V.P. investigators, historical and modern [7].

In his article entitled, "Formation of Electronic Phenomena," Tom Butler, co-director of the AAEVP, suggests that the use of low powered field effect transistor (FET) in early IC recorders may have contributed to the ability of these recorders to successfully capture E.V.P. He suggests that the performance of vacuum tube recorders and IC recorders, using low powered FET, are very similar. This similarity in the active region of the electronic circuit of both vacuum tube and IC recorders may be the reason both of these recording systems seem to collect more E.V.P. then the bipolar transistor system of modern cassette recorders [5].

Sound and recording quality varies greatly in IC recorders. Most IC recorders come with different recording modes to choose from. There are usually three: standard play (SP), fine quality (FQ) and high quality (HQ). Using an SP recording mode gives you the longest recording time but the poorest sound quality, while HQ will sizably reduce your recording time but give you better sound quality. The differences in the sound quality of these modes can be great. Some researchers say that recording in SP will give you the built in white noise effect that is claimed to be needed for spirits to put voices on recorders. Others discount the need for white noise and favor the clarity of the HQ mode. Be aware that SP mode in some recorders is so poor that without a good quality backup recording it would be hard to determine whether an E.V.P. is just that or actually a normal sound that is inferiorly recorded. Experimenters need to listen to the sound qualities in each recording mode to determine which will be acceptable for E.V.P. recordings.

Not all E.V.P. investigators today like IC recorders. There are E.V.P. investigators who continue to favor vacuum tube reel-to-reel recorders, and those who use cassettes and obtain outstanding results with them. As of yet, no one has definitively determined how the voices get onto the recording devices but what is known is that E.V.P. can be obtained using both magnetic tape and digital technology.

The role of a microphone is to convert sound waves in the air into electrical signals. The E.V.P. investigator has the choice of using the internal microphone built into most recorders or to use an external microphone. The use of the internal microphones on cassette recorders has long been discouraged because of the ability of the built in microphones to pick up the sound of the gears and motors of the recorder. In this case, this internal recording noise is not a good background sound source and could actually drown out possible E.V.P. To eliminate this problem an external microphone can be used.

IC recorders have no gear or motor noise to deal with, so one can use the built in microphones of these recorders. But many investigators prefer the clarity and wide frequency range that a quality microphone can offer, even with IC recorders. Investigators can choose from omnidirectional microphones that pick up sound waves from almost all directions or unidirectional microphones that are sensitive to sound from only one direction. As stated earlier, consideration must be given to the possibility that external microphone cables can act like an antenna.

It has been suggested by some researchers that E.V.P. utterances bypass the microphone and are imprinted directly onto the recording device. Several groups have experimented with this hypothesis and the results are mixed.

An experiment conducted by Euvaldo Cabral concluded that E.V.P. voices were produced not by an acoustic effect, but by an electrical effect. In his experiment he used six microphones that were sampled electronically. His results showed that only one microphone was affected. If an acoustic signal had been involved all six microphones would have been affected.

Prompted by Cabral's experiment, Alexander MacRae conducted his own experiment using his Alpha Interface System, a receiver and two microphones. Alexander MacRae's Alpha device is a unique system that originally was a biofeedback device with Galvanic Skin Response (GSR) capability. Changes in the GSR were indicated by light and tone changes. Modifications to its design have resulted in a device that is successfully used to capture E.V.P. [7]. For MacRae's experiment he documented under what conditions E.V.P. were obtained when the equipment used for the experiment was on or off. He only received E.V.P. when the Alpha System was switched on and was operated at the same time the receiver and microphones were on. He noted that E.V.P. levels remained equal in both channels even when one microphone was shielded from any electrical charge. But when one microphone was wrapped in acoustic insulating material there was a fall off in the response from that microphone. He concluded that E.V.P., in its Alpha Interface System version, was an acoustic rather then electrical effect [22].

Some researchers continue to experiment with the diode method made famous by Konstantine Raudive. These diode recordings were done with an enclosed, germanium diode circuit connected to a 6-8 cm antenna [28]. When this diode was plugged into the microphone input of the recorder and the volume of the recorder turned up all the way, Raudive was able to record voices he said, "come nearest to those of ordinary human ones" [28].

Germanium diode recordings do not pick up any of the audible sound from the area of the recording but do transmit electrical signals.

Recording and Editing

Although these human, location and environmental factors and the equipment used for E.V.P. apply to all types of E.V.P. recording, the field investigators faces unique challenges. Field investigators are expected to adjust to new conditions with each different investigation location. This can be challenging at times but there are ways an investigator can control the E.V.P. session that can make these challenges manageable.

First, clean recording techniques are essential in these changing situations. Setting the recorder and the external microphone, if used, down during recording can eliminate unintentional noise. Going one step further and placing the recorders on a padded surface and the microphone in a stand can reduce reverberation. Many things, including the surface you put your recorder on, can cause this reverberation.

Carrying recorders while recording during an investigation can result in picking up extraneous sounds caused by things as mundane as walking or rubbing fingers across the recorder. These extra noises can contaminate a recording, are annoying to listen to on playback, and sometimes are mistaken for E.V.P.

When doing outdoors investigations, a wind screen on a microphone will help cut down on wind noise. The location of the recorder and microphone during breezy weather is also important. Don't record into the wind and try to find a sheltered area. Be aware of where you are and voice mark it. Noises such as flowing water or people talking in the background, though obvious at the time, are easily forgotten when listening to the recording.

When working with a team on an investigation, make sure all the people involved, including clients and any other attendees, know they must stay quiet during the recording. If they make a noise such as cough or whisper they must say that they did so. All present in the session, including the facilitator, must voice mark any event like this. It is very easy to forget these little incidents and later think a faint whisper is a paranormal event instead of a human whisper that wasn't voice marked.

Aside from the noise that can be generated from people at the investigation location, the location itself can be noisy. The houses and businesses of onsite investigations are already primed with the noise of air conditioners, furnace blowers, appliance sounds and outside noises filtering in. Closing windows and turning off loud equipment and fans, when possible, can help to establish a proper sound to noise ratio during the recording session.

As stated earlier, some in the E.V.P. community believe a carrier wave produced by a background noise source is needed for spirits to be able to produce a voice that can be recorded. But too much background noise will only mask E.V.P. and make listening to the playback of the recording difficult. For recording done in a quiet, controlled location, there are several downloads available that provide a wide variety of background sound sources that individuals, interested in this method, may want to try. Alexander MacRae offers a download that includes white and pink noise, the sound of a water fall, a burning bush and a recording of the noise produced by the Spiricom. Stefan Bion's EVPmaker is available as freeware and Sonia Rinaldi has made available a download of Portuguese language crowd babble that has been clipped of all recognizable sounds.

Backup documentation is very important in all E.V.P. recordings. Besides being a possible source of collaborated data, backup recordings, videos and written notes can assist in deciding what is or isn't an E.V.P. during analysis. One way to double check a suspected E.V.P. is to record with two recorders simultaneously. In addition to your E.V.P. recorder, especially if it is an IC reorder, record with a good quality cassette recorder or computer. Cassette and computer recordings will have better sound quality then a recording from a small IC recorder. These clean recordings may expose the real nature of sounds that could easily be mistaken for paranormal sounds. It is also suggested by some in the E.V.P. community that if you capture the same E.V.P. on two recorders it most likely is not paranormal in nature. The consistent use of backup recordings during investigations will help researchers determined if this is actually true in all cases.

Video taping sessions also can help establish the true nature of questionable E.V.P. voices. Aside from acting like a second recorder, a tape also supplies visual evidence that might be helpful when collaborating evidence. Once again, even the most cautious investigator's memory, of even recent events, is by nature fallible.

Lastly, during investigations, written notes are helpful. Noting times questions were asked, listing who is present and documenting environmental conditions can all be crucial information. The goal of the paranormal investigator is to be as certain as possible that the evidence presented of a paranormal event is, in fact, just that. Careful record keeping is essential to this process.

In a controlled E.V.P. session, a script of prepared questions, read by one person, could be used. This allows control of the question asking portion of the session but it also can set up questions that, if answered, can be evidential of the suspected haunting. It is a matter of policy in the S.W.P.R.G. that as few people as possible know ahead of time the story and source of paranormal activity associated with an investigation. This keeps investigators from subconsciously trying to fit evidence into the story of the investigation. For example, if someone from the E.V.P. team picks up a voice that is later analyzed as saying "Amy," and we find out that the client's Aunt Amy died in the house, this is very evidential. Since the name wasn't known at the time of recording or during analysis, it wasn't subconsciously or consciously being listened for. A script can have key questions that pertain to certain events of the haunting but not enough information to give away too much information to other investigators.

A freeform session where anyone can ask questions may need more voice marking and note taking, but is usually much more energetic and interesting then a scripted session. Control questions can also be asked during this type of session.

Some investigators use VOR, or the Voice Operated Recording system found on recorders. The idea behind the VOR system is that the recorder will only start recording when a sound activates it and will turn off after the sound stops. That this can cut down a 30 minute recording session to five minutes is attractive when one considers the time it would take to analyze 30 minute of recording. But questions arise about this system that may suggest that, although it may be suitable for individuals that only record in one controlled location, it isn't the best for field investigations. The need for keeping track of what is going on is crucial for verification of anything collected during a field investigation. That sometimes means knowing what was happening in the big picture. A recording of the complete session, not just the questions, extra noises and suspected E.V.P., will supply continuity to what happened during the session. Additionally, field investigations with multiple investigators will generate noise that would keep the unit popping on and off constantly. This could be annoying during playback. Activating the VOR switch might be something one would consider when setting the recorder in an isolated area and leaving it on. But even this scenario would warrant back up with a video camera or another recorder to record the whole event and would need to be reviewed.

The E.V.P. sessions are the quickest part of the process. Recording analysis, on the other hand, can take a great deal of time and patience.

This process entails listening to the recording, noting suspected areas, analyzing them through computer editing, interpreting what the E.V.P. utterance says, having others scrutinize the E.V.P. and the interpretation and finally checking the suspected E.V.P. against other data.

Listening to the recording needs to be done through headphones. Noise canceling headphones or heavily insulated headphones like those used by car racing pit crews work very well. If you are going to listen to the recording directly off the recorder, a mono headphone will let the recording come through both earpieces where stereo headphones will be limited to only one ear piece. Many investigators transfer the complete recording session to a computer, convert it to stereo mode, and proceed with their analysis using standard stereo headphones.

Listen to the complete session recording in a quiet location without any distractions. During the initial listen-through mark down the time or counter number of any suspected E.V.P. When going back to listen to these suspected segments, listen not just to the suspected E.V.P., but also to several seconds before it and several seconds after it. The sound of the suspected E.V.P. needs to be compared to normal sounds in the recording that may have occurred during these times.

At this point the suspected E.V.P. should be compared to your backup recording to determine if the E.V.P. is possibly distorted noise or the muffled voice of another investigator. It may be possible to pick up the same E.V.P. on the backup recorder. If it is believed this is the case, check any other audio that may have been recording in the same location at the same time. This could be video or a computer monitoring system. This will help determine if the E.V.P. was caught on multiple recorders.

Audio files will need to be made of the original E.V.P. and any backup recordings. When transferring these recording to a computer audio program make these first recordings include a few seconds before the E.V.P. and a few seconds after it. A copy of the original E.V.P., unedited, as it was heard in context will prove useful. This will be the original audio file you will keep a copy of and use to compare edited versions to.

Editing of suspected E.V.P. is a learned skill that can take a lot of time to understand and master. Although there are some sound engineers who have gone into E.V.P. investigation and analysis, and have added much to the knowledge of E.V.P. editing, it is not necessary to be a sound engineer to be able to edit effectively.

The first hurdle in editing is deciding what audio editing programs to use. Adobe Audition is a popular program that many E.V.P. researchers use.

DC Six Audio Work Station by Tracer Technologies offers audio forensic tools as well as a variety of audio restoration, enhancement and editing tools. There are some free downloadable audio editors such as Audacity and some modestly priced ones such as AVS Audio Tools, Acoustica, and Goldwave. There are also some specialized programs that suit E.V.P. editing. One is Clear Voice Denoiser, which is only a noise reduction program and the other is The Amazing Slow Downer, which as its name implies, will slow down recordings. Both are available in a free demo version.

The basic editing process for E.V.P. is already well documented so one can find tutorials on E.V.P. audio editing by searching the internet. Some sites are free while others require a fee. Individuals and organizations are also offering classes and E.V.P. certification programs. With either a class or certification programs remember that although there are many experienced E.V.P. researchers around, there is no one person or organization that is the ultimate authority on E.V.P.

Some E.V.P. books offer basic recording and editing information as well. *There is No Death and There Are No Dead,* by Tom and Lisa Butler and *Speak with the Dead: Seven Methods for Spirit Communication,* by Konstantinos give step-by-step recording and editing directions.

Caution must be advised at this point. Editing tools can easily be overused when trying to clean up an E.V.P. example. It is best not to get heavy handed and to let a suspected E.V.P. go rather then to force it into something that may resemble a voice. IC recorders are known to distort normally produced sounds into ones that can easily be mistaken for E.V.P. It is easy to manipulate these sounds using an editing program enough to change a natural sound into a sound that strongly resembles a voice. This is one reason some E.V.P. researchers discourage editing, enhancing or manipulation suspected E.V.P. voices in any way.

Edited or not, a suspected E.V.P. will need to be interpreted. If the E.V.P. is of A quality this part of the process should not present much of a problem. But class B or C E.V.P. are another matter and care will need to be taken to listen carefully.

Alexander MacRae spent much of his life engaged in speech and hearing research. He wrote an excellent section in his book, *E.V.P. and New Dimensions,* about the hearing and listening challenges that investigators face when working with E.V.P. Some people have better hearing than others, but since hearing deficiencies usually progress slowly over many years, many people do not realize that their hearing is sub-standard. High frequencies disappear first, then words become muffled, and the brain attempts to make sense of what is heard. Also accents, dialects, and familiarity with one's own way of speaking can influence what is heard. If the signal to noise ratio is too high because the environmental background sound is loud, no matter how good the E.V.P. is, it probably will not be able to be understood [21].

When making an interpretation, think phonetically. Instead of getting caught up in what is heard as a complete phrase, test the sounds in the E.V.P. against consonant and vowel sounds and write out exactly what you hear phonetically. Another option is to use a software program designed to analyze speech phonetically.

Make sure that sections of the E.V.P. that are actually missing, masked in noise or faded out near the end, are not given meaning. The brain will try to make sense of these obscured areas and will want to complete the phrase.

Once an E.V.P. is interpreted, it is hard not to hear that interpretation. The disbelief that others can't hear what was perceived as a clear voice can be disappointing. And it can be maddening when another interpretation of the same E.V.P. is offered that isn't even phonetically close to the original interpretation. Going back and listening to E.V.P. a few days after the initial editing and interpretation can sometimes reveal that the E.V.P. isn't nearly as clear as was originally thought. Without the use of written records or prompts, approach this second listen through as if hearing the E.V.P. for the first time. Chances are if the E.V.P. is easily understood, most people will be able to hear it also.

Another step in the interpretation process can be the hardest, as the E.V.P. discovered during the investigation is offered to others for critique. Not revealing the original interpretation until others have had a time to make their own interpretations is essential. It is too easy to take the interpretation of someone else and hear only that. The goal is to see if all members of a listening panel hear the same thing or at least come phonetically close to one another's interpretations.

When offering E.V.P. audio files to others to listen to it is suggested to offer the E.V.P. in two forms. The first is a file that shows the E.V.P. in context. This file would include what was recorded just before and after the E.V.P. It is often easier to initially hear and understand E.V.P. in this format. The next form would be a file that contains only the E.V.P.

The next part of investigative E.V.P. analysis is comparing what you decide is an E.V.P. to other data collected during the investigation. This is where knowing the time and location that the E.V.P. was caught is important.

Depending on the data collection systems used during the investigation one could detect other events that may have happened in the environment at that time. This could include EMF readings, radiation, temperature and personal experiences.

Although this long process may seem redundant, tedious, and time consuming, it is important to ensure that what is offered to a client and the paranormal community is as accurate as possible.

E.V.P. Research

Aside from individuals who record exclusively in one location or haunted location investigators, there are a growing number of individuals who are now conducting laboratory research and experimentation into E.V.P.

As stated before, Alexander MacRae has done research into E.V.P. using his Alpha Interface System. To address the claim that all E.V.P. are stray radio pickups, he conducted an experiment in a radio and sound wave shielded room provided by the Institute of Noetic Sciences. The experiment in the double shielded room resulted in the successful pick up of E.V.P. voices [21].

The Interdisciplinary Laboratory for Biopsychocybernetics Research or Il Labratori, in Italy is dedicated to scientific research into paranormal phenomena. Paolo Presi, an aeronautical engineer, is the director of E.V.P. research. He, along with electronic engineer and expert in voice identification Daniele Gulla, and director of the research department at IL Labratorio Michele Dinacastro, are conducting research into the analysis of the electro-acoustical structure of E.V.P. utterances [25].

Other E.V.P. researchers around the world have contributed to the understanding of E.V.P. and to the tools available to utilize in this discipline. Stefan Bion developed the software called EVPmaker. This system generates "acoustic raw material" by dividing "any recording of speech into short segments and then plays them back continuously in random order" [3]. Some researchers have found this system useful as a background sound source.

Organizations are also trying to advance understanding by conducting experiments. The American Association of Electronic Voice Phenomena has an ongoing experiment called the 4Cell Demonstration. Each member within a 4Cell team has a job as a requester, sender, receiver or scribe. The requester thinks of a question and relays it to the sender who then asks that question and request that the answer be put on the receiver's recorder. The receiver is the only one who records an E.V.P. session and asks for the answer to the question. The receiver will then listen to the recording and send any suspected E.V.P. to the scribe. The scribe then makes a determination of the interpretation of any suspected E.V.P. After this the scribe ask the receiver what the question was and the group determines if an answer to the question was found in the captured E.V.P. (AAEVP, 4Cell).

Although this type of research and development is essential to the understanding of E.V.P., the future of E.V.P. doesn't rest exclusively in the hands of individuals doing laboratory research. Few scientists in the areas of physics, engineering or psychology have expressed an interest in the study of E.V.P. and the paranormal field at large. Even in parapsychology E.V.P. study is often dismissed. It will inevitably be through careful experimentation and documentation by the layperson that the study of E.V.P. will become of interest to the scientific community.

The Future of E.V.P.—Conclusion

In the year 1959 when Friedrich Juergenson recorded his first E.V.P. voice, American Airlines started the first passenger plane service across the United States, NASA selected seven astronauts for the Mercury program, Rod Serling's "The Twilight Zone" made its debut, and Texas Instruments requested a patent for the integrated circuit [27]. In the almost 50 years since then, international air travel has become an everyday occurrence, human space exploration has advanced past the Mercury missions into Gemini, Apollo, the Space Shuttle and now the Ares rockets which plan to carry the next exploration vehicles to the moon and Mars. Some of the science fiction of early television and cinema has become a reality, and the integrated circuit forever changed society. Has the research into E.V.P. kept pace with these other momentous changes? Certainly, as technology has advanced so has the equipment E.V.P. investigators have used. Some equipment, like IC recorders, show evidence of being exceptionally conducive to E.V.P. recording. Computers allow for the use of audio editing programs to clean up E.V.P. in a way early researchers could not. And the internet has made it easy to share E.V.P. files and information. Today E.V.P. are recorded by thousands of individuals who are associated with ghost hunting and paranormal investigation groups as well as those who come to the recording of E.V.P. for personal or spiritual reasons. The sheer numbers of those interested in E.V.P. will spur on the research and discoveries that will advance the chances of understanding this intriguing phenomenon.

Section VI

PARANORMAL INVESTIGATION, INFORMATION AND PROCESS

Chapter 9

SPECIALISTS WITHIN YOUR ORGANIZATION

Within every great organization there should be specialists. These are people who know a great deal about a specific field. There are a variety of different areas you will need your organization to cover. We have listed some, but there may be other areas that you will find you may need and some you may not. Many new organizations will not have specialists to begin with, and this is understandable. Your goal then is to assign specific areas to your members to research and learn about so they may be able to bring their knowledge about that area to the group. Remember to make sure that you assign specific areas to people who have an interest in them. As you can see, we never use the term "Expert" because we believe there are NO "Experts" in the field of Paranormal Research, only specialists in their specific areas of interest.

The Director:

The Director is the person that oversees EVERY aspect of your organization. This includes but is not limited to: investigations, member management, media appearances & press opportunities, organizational processes & procedures, training, special events, promotions and fund raisers, purchases and much more. Generally, but not always, the person or persons who founded or organized your group will take over this responsibility.

Client Care Specialist:

This person should be the initial contact for your client. They are responsible for being present at both the preliminary & full investigations, not only to represent the clients best interest, but to explain to the client the procedures taking place and help them understand what the investigators are doing, why they are doing it and how it is being done.

Lead Investigator:

This person oversees the entire investigation process. They make sure everything is being done properly, on time and under controlled conditions. This includes the investigators, equipment placement, client care, data collection, time management and much more. All investigators report to this person during an investigation. The lead investigator is responsible for gathering all of the information from the investigators and creating a formal report for the clients.

Case Manager:

This person is in charge of retaining all of the paperwork and records for each investigation. This includes keeping a file of each investigation with all of the client's signed waivers, CD's of investigation data, the completed investigation report, and any audio/video that was captured during the investigation.

Parapsychology Specialist:

This person would be responsible for being well informed about the field, ideas, concepts, hypotheses and theories in the field of parapsychology. For the reasons discussed earlier in the book it is essential that all people in the group have a firm understanding of parapsychology. Since there is a lot of material to read and keep up on it would be beneficial to have someone within the group keep an eye on the literature and share relevant information with the rest of the group.

E.V.P. Specialist:

An E.V.P. specialist doesn't spend most of their time recording E.V.P. but instead spends vast amounts of time listening to and analyzing the recording sessions. These time intensive tasks not only require a good ear and tempered editing skills but also good record keeping to assist in the collaboration of other data. While on an investigation, other team members may record for E.V.P. but it is the E.V.P. specialist's responsibility to conduct several controlled and well monitored sessions. This may include setting up a recording area, recording simultaneously with several recorders, and keeping track of what happens during the recording sessions. E.V.P. is an area of paranormal research whose results can often be subjective. An important goal of an E.V.P. specialist is to attempt to eliminate as many variables in the recording and editing process as possible to assist in the verification of suspected E.V.P.

Equipment Specialist / Technical Engineer:

Depending upon how many people you have and their qualifications, this can be either a one or two person job. The Equipment Specialist should have a strong working knowledge of all of the equipment in your arsenal. He/she should not only know how it works, but how to use it properly, what it detects, how it detects it, how to analyze what it has detected and how to find natural explanations for readings. The Technical Engineer should know the equipment backwards and forwards, but this person should also know how to fix the equipment and customize or manipulate it electronically for other uses. (i.e. a handheld tri-field meter needs to be adapted to collect data and download it onto a computer).

Technical Assistant/s:

These people help the Equipment Specialist with any technical assistance they need. Placing equipment such as cameras or audio equipment is a specific area or simply unrolling or rolling up wiring. These people as well as the Equipment Specialist should be the only ones handling the stationary equipment such as the camera system or other highly expensive equipment. This does not include hand-held equipment such as EMF detectors or Non-Contact thermal scanners . . . which everyone should handle.

Historical Research Specialist:

This specialist works on the historical factors of an investigation. They will talk to the homeowners/business owners to find any factual information on a dwelling. They will also go to the public library and research any information they can including census records, birth & death records, fire or other property damage records, new construction (permits) etc. and find out everything they need to know about the history of a specific home or area.

Photography / Video Specialist:

This person is very important to a professional investigation team. Some groups may have a member who is really good or enjoys photography/videography and some may not. The groups who do not have a member who is good or interested in this area will have to go to an outside source for their photography/videography information. A good place to find a person who would be a great asset to your group would be someone who works for a professional photography business such as Kodak, Fuji Film, or any local companies or professional photographers. If you tell them what you are doing, you may find that they are very willing to help.

Chapter 10

THE INVESTIGATION PROCESS
From start to finish—What's involved?

Knowing how to investigate a haunting is one thing, but not many realize how important it is to keep structure and consistency during investigations. Our main goals as paranormal investigators are to research, investigate and document paranormal activity. To be consistent and as accurate as possible while doing this, we need to know exactly what we are looking for and what we need to do to get results. By being consistent and following a structure the members of your team will not only look professional and competent, but will BE professional and competent. Every member of your team should know the exact process to which an investigation needs to be performed. Each team member needs to be assigned his or her task in the investigation and be responsible for the completion, follow through and reporting of his or her task.

Initial Contact Stage

More than likely, if your group is like ours, you probably either get a call or an email from a homeowner or business owner with claims of hauntings, ghosts or some other type of paranormal activity going on at a specific location. When this happens, you need to realize that the reason these people are calling you is because they are either curious, frightened or possibly at the end of their ropes . . . and need some answers.

They look to you for answers, but first we need to listen. Listen to what they are relaying to you, how they present their information, their experiences, and what their reason was for contacting you. Do they want you to get rid of the ghost? Do they just want to understand what's going on? Is it a way for them to get attention? Knowing who these people are and what their intentions are will also help your investigation considerably.

The S.W.P.R.G. has developed an initial set of questions that we require all clients to answer completely before we will consider conducting an investigation. We have added a few sample questions at the end of this chapter as an example. We would recommend you come up with a list of questions that you feel you need to know in order to get an idea of what type of activity is going on. Just a variety of different questions that you, as an investigator, can refer back to when needed. If you ask the right questions, you can get answers into many areas such as the location of the reported activity, a person's belief system and many other important areas of interest that might open up the doorway to all your answers.

The Preliminary Visit
(*or Pre-Investigation*)

The pre-investigation stage is a very important part of the process. It provides you with a large amount of information that you will need to determine if a full investigation will be necessary. This stage takes anywhere from one to two hours and only requires two investigators on the scene. This stage consists of the following steps:

1. **Take a tour of the location**—Videotape the tour while the property owner details the accounts of paranormal activity they have witnessed on the premises. Videotaping is necessary and will easily allow you to get a full view of the premises. You will be able to reference this tape in the future when it's time to set up your equipment, cameras, and decide where to place your investigators if a full investigation if deemed necessary.

2. **Videotape interviews with the witnesses**—Talk to anyone who has experienced activity first hand at the location. Videotape your conversations with them while they describe their experiences to you. By taping their experiences, this allows you to go back and review their information after you analyze your findings. This will allow you to note any correlations between personal experiences and the data you've collected and also allows you to find similarities between witness's experiences or to determine the occurance of natural phenomena.

Make sure you review this videotape fully. If you're lucky, you may even catch something "paranormal" on tape during this stage. We can assure you that this *has* happened to us before!!

3. **Take baseline readings**—Taking environmental readings during this stage will allow you to understand and document the full range of natural and man-made power sources and other activity coming from the property. Environmental information that should be tracked are:

   • Natural & man-made electromagnetic fields (EMF)
   • Positive and negative ion counts
   • Radiation
   • Temperature
   • Static electricity

   Investigators personal interpretations should also be noted at this time.

4. **Try to find natural explanations**—This is where your credibility comes in. Trying to find natural explanation's for reported paranormal activity is EXTREMELY important. If a squeak is heard in a specific location every night, there is a great possibility that there is a natural explanation for it. Try to find it!!! Use deductive reasoning and an open mind and you will do great! Remember this famous quote—***Occam's Razor states***:

   "All things being equal,
   the simplest answer is usually the right one".

5. **Evaluate the preliminary investigation to determine if a full investigation is warranted**—After the pre-investigation, it will be very important to look over all of the results to determine whether a full investigation is necessary. You will need to take into consideration the people involved in the reported haunting. The eye-witnesses, home owners, etc. How are they responding to the activity they have reported? Are they in desperate need of your help? If so, this should be a very important part of your decision. Since you are providing a community service, this would be a very important part of your decision to do the investigation. If, after talking to the individuals involved you notice that they are just interested in watching you and having fun with it, and if

the data documented in the pre is not significant, you can choose not to proceed with the full investigation. Investigations are very time consuming and costly for everyone involved so each and every investigation you do needs to be decided upon by your group or the director.

The Investigation

The investigation process is probably the MOST important of them all. In order to get the best and cleanest data you can get, it is very important that all of the processes be followed.

Evaluate the Investigation Site:

The first thing you need to do is decide how many investigators you are going to need to cover the investigation site. A two-bedroom apartment will only need about three investigators whereas a four-bedroom two-story house may need five or six to entirely cover the area. Coordinate your investigators by what they are good at. (Example: If Cindy is good at E.V.P., make sure Cindy can be there or someone else who knows how to collect E.V.P. as cleanly and accurately as Cindy). Keep in mind though, the more investigators you have, the harder it is to control your surroundings and the more work that needs to be done.

Control Your Conditions:

It is very important to know that the data you collect is as clean and accurate as possible. In order to get this clean and accurate data, you need to be able to control your conditions during your investigation. What this means is, if someone walks past an EMF detector while it is being data logged onto a computer, chances are that it picked up that person's own natural EMF field and data logged it. In that case, you need to make sure that you note any activity along with the date and time in a log so that you can reference it later when you are analyzing the data. We would HIGHLY recommend videotaping the area where you are data logging information as a reference point. Make sure that the clock on the videotape is the same as on your computer.

Client Care:

You will need to make the client aware of the entire process. This includes how many investigators will be on site, how long the investigation will take (approximately), what the processes are, what you plan on doing, and how you plan on doing it. Do you plan on bringing the client into the investigation? Some groups do, some don't. We recommend that you do involve the client in the investigation process. Bring them in on E.V.P. sessions. Explain to them anything they want to know.

What Equipment Should You Use?:

You will want to use only equipment that will be useful for your investigation. Using all of your equipment during one investigation may not always prove to be useful or even wise. For example, using a motion detector outside wouldn't be that useful to you since the thing would go off ever time a leaf blew by, so be aware of the conditions around you. Many times different pieces of equipment will set off other equipment so be aware of that. We know there have been many times when a new member would be holding onto their camera and a gauss meter at the same time and accidentally get them too close. When this happens, the EMF detector goes off and they start getting all excited thinking they got something, when in fact it's their own digital camera putting out enough EMFs to set it off. BE AWARE OF YOUR SURROUNDINGS!!! We can't state this enough!

Setting Up Your Equipment and Video Cameras:

Taking readings in locations where things area said to happen AND in locations where people are at when they are experiencing the activity will allow you possibly uncover an explanation for the experiences. Listen carefully to what the witnesses are telling you. This will give you insight of where your best options would be for detecting paranormal activity.

Mapping:

Besides videotaping the dwelling during the pre-investigation, drawing a map of the entire location is also necessary. At the same time the stationary equipment is being set-up (cameras, etc.), the mapper and sweeps team sets off to map out the location. The mapper and the sweeps team will work in conjunction to make note of any valuable information as to natural or strange environmental readings in the location before the investigation officially begins. The mapper will map out each floor individually and make note of any natural sources of energy (such as where the fuse box is located, electrical outlets, etc) or any strange or unusual readings the sweeps team will pick up during their walk-through.

Sweeps:

Keeping track of environmental readings throughout an investigation is very important. Sweeps will allow you to do this. By using handheld equipment such as EMF detectors, ambient air thermometers, non-contact thermoscanners, and even tri-field meters you will be able to note any changes in the environment. Using the map that was drawn during the beginning of the investigation, you can go through each room individually with your equipment and note any changes in readings. Use the map to note any natural or unusual changes in an area. These areas should be noted on the map itself. Sweeps should be done at least once every two hours.

Quiet Observation:

Now is the time to position your investigators in different rooms/areas of the dwelling, sit down somewhere, get comfortable, leave the data logging equipment going in a place where activity has been reported, leave your video & audio recorders going, turn off all of the lights and turn on all your natural senses. Sit with the lights out for about half an hour while you look, listen, feel and sense the environment around you. Make note of anything unusual you experience at this point.

E.V.P. Sessions:

During E.V.P. sessions, make sure to verbally note on the recorder any sounds you hear during your session. This will make analyzing the audio much easier and if you do pick up some strange voice and didn't hear it at the time, you will be assured of what you captured. We would also recommend videotaping E.V.P. sessions as a backup to the audio that you capture and also to visually detect any natural occurrences of unusual sounds such as someone shifting in their chair and a strange sound was heard at the same time. For more information on E.V.P., see chapter 8 "E.V.P.—An Overview"

Review data/video/audio:

For every hour of data/video/audio you collect, you will need to analyze every hour. Most of the time, you will have several cameras recording at the same time. For every camera you have recording video, you will have to watch every minute of every video recorded. Same goes for audio and data collection. We recommend having several members of your team watch different cameras rather than one person watching many. This is, of course, dependent upon the equipment you have.

Evidence Correlation:

Correlating environmental data together as well as to subjective paranormal experiences is essential if we are to truly understand what might be happening at a given location. This is why data logging with date/time stamps and taking detailed notes is essential during the investigation. If one investigator has an experience, records an E.V.P., or captures something on video, we can go to the data and see if there were any environmental changes at the same time. Having more than once piece of data provides better evidence that something changed in the environment that may or may not have been paranormal. The best case is if someone had a paranormal experience at the same time a change in one or more environmental conditions was recorded. This will help us collect the needed data in order to better understand the phenomena.

Therefore, it is essential that everyone keep accurate and detailed notes during the investigation. Also be sure that all of the clocks on your video, E.V.P. recorders, computers and other equipment are synced. This will allow you to compare all of your different data to see if there are any correlations.

The Reveal

Revealing the findings to the homeowners/business owners is a very delicate situation. You want to let them know everything you find, but the important part is that you need to make them understand everything you are telling them. You wouldn't want them to assume there is a strange, mysterious phantom ghost lurking around their basement when you found out it's only their fuse box giving off large amounts of EMF. Giving them the information is only part of the process . . . . make them understand what your findings mean.

Charging for Investigations

There has been a lot of controversy surrounding groups that charge for investigations . . . but this does seem to be a double-edged sword. Where psychics seem to be able to charge anything they want for a "reading", paranormal investigators get criticized for charging to do actual work during an investigation. I know this seems wrong, but this is where your credibility comes in to play. Knowing that you are a professional, credible paranormal research organization your true profits will come from your name and your reputation as a serious and credible paranormal research group. Soon, your profits will not need to come from doing investigations, rather your services will be profitable as you begin to charge for speaking engagements, technical consulting and other professional services. Keep up the great work, and you will become very successful!!

Sample Set of Questions

The following is a sample of the questions we ask potential clients:

1   *Please give a general description of the occurrences.*
2   *Please give the names and ages of all those living/working in the situation where the activity have taken place.*
3   *Please give the educational background of all those in the location.*
4   *How long have you lived/worked there?*
5   *Any disturbances noted at previous addresses?*
6   *When did the current disturbances begin?*
7   *When was the most recent incident?*
8   *Would you say the occurrences are frequent? Are they occurring with any apparent regularity?*
9   *Have the disturbances been increasing in frequency and severity since they first begin?*
10   *Who are those people directly involved? What did they experience?*
11   *Have you looked for ordinary, normal explanations? What makes you sure the events are paranormal?*
12   *What kinds of books or articles have you read about psychic phenomena or the occult/supernatural/unsolved mysteries?*
13   *What are your feelings/beliefs regarding psychic phenomena or the spiritual world? What is your religious background (both family and your present religious status)?*
14   *What would you like done to help you?*
15   *Would you allow me and perhaps some colleagues to do a serious investigation of the occurrences in your home/office?*

Chapter 11

S.W.P.R.G. CASE FILES

Documenting case files are very important to any investigation group. The following case files are just a few that the S.W.P.R.G. has investigated. Some you will find on our website at *www.SWPRG.com*, while others are exclusive to this book.

A variety of different equipment is used by the S.W.P.R.G. during investigations. The following is a list of the equipment the S.W.P.R.G. has at their disposal. Not every piece specified below is used during every investigation, but the findings for each piece used are listed in each report.

- Color Led Infrared Video Camera (x8)
- Lorex L124A-81 4 channel DVR with 80GB hard drive
- Fuji finepix S7000 digital camera
- Radio Shack boundary condenser microphone (omni directional) *33-3022*
- Panasonic RR-US360 Digital Recorder
- Sony TCM-200DV Cassette Recorder
- Non-Contact IR Thermal Probe Scanner
- Tri-field Natural EMF Meter (x2)
- Tri-field Meter (x2)
- Temperature Gauge (x2)
- EMF Gauss Meter (x2)
- Apple G4 Laptop
- Radio Frequency Counter

- Hall Effect Gauss meter from Integrity Design and Research Corporation (IDR-309). A bare probe was used with the gauss meter. The bandwidth of the bare probe is 68Hz at 3dB
- Air Ion Counter, Positive and negative ion counts are displayed as ions/cm3
- Sony Digital Handycam *DCR-TRV19 NTSC* with night shot
- Olympus Camedia Digital Camera C-4000 zoom. 4.0 mega pixel
- GE Personal Portable Recorder and Cassette Player *3-5027*

The D.E.A.D.© System
(Direct Environmental Acquisition Data logging system)

- Triaxial ELF magnetic field meter with pc interface. The bandwidth is 30Hz to 2000Hz and an accuracy of +/-3% at 50Hz/60Hz and +/-5% at 40 to 200Hz. Data is logged using the supplied software.
- HOBO Temperature data logger from Onset Computer Corporation with data logging and archiving ability. Onset Computer Corporation provided software is used for data logging and archiving.
- GM-10 radiation detector from Black Cat Systems with pc interface. The Radiation Acquisition and Display (RAD) Software is used to log and archive the data. Radiation detected includes alpha, beta, and gamma/x-ray. Data is displayed as counts per minute (cpm).
- Averatec AV3715 laptop computer.
- Tri-field natural EMF meter modified to be data logged by the HOBO data logger.
- Fluxgate Magnetometer Model 539 with APS software. Set to collect approximately 400 samples per second. Data is analyzed using SigView.

~ All equipment is calibrated and tested prior to use according to manufacture specifications.

Photo courtesy of Deb Skinvik

THE BAR NEXT DOOR
232 E. Olin Avenue
Madison, WI

Date: December 12, 2004

Investigators: Derek Arneson, Walt Baker, Tim Buchholz, Chris Carter, Troy Hartman, Jennifer Lauer, Alicia Sanders, Dave Schumacher, Deb Skinvik.

Cause for the Investigation:

The Manager of the Bar Next Door, Kristin Olshanski, contacted us to investigate a possible haunting. Kristen claimed that other employees, patrons of the bar, and she had been experiencing strange incidents. Occurrences reported included a feeling of being followed in stairwells, the sound of footsteps descending the staircase after hours, unexplained noises of loud thuds and rattling glasses, lights turning on and off, unexplained smells of body odor, citrus, and mustiness that last for one hour and then dissipate, shadows of people being seen by customers, ex-employees seeing a man in a fedora and long coat and a woman with long red hair and white dress during closed hours, portraits, bottles, and cigar boxes falling off of walls and secured shelves, doors slamming closed, being poked in the back when alone in a room, chairs found in a different location and position other than when last placed after hours.

The History:

In the 1930's there was an Irish family from Chicago's Northwest side; Roger "The Terrible" Tuohey, arch foe of Al Capone, his brother Eddie and two sisters. Capone was too powerful for Tuohey so Tuohey opened up roadhouses away from Chicago to distribute his beer. One of these roadhouses was The Wonder Bar. This was the distribution center to supply illegal alcohol for most of Wisconsin. The Wonder Bar became a safe-house for gangsters traveling in and out of the area. A secret tunnel was put in underground for a fast getaway if needed. The building was built bullet-proof with hidden compartments. Purportedly, there is a body buried behind the fireplace in the second floor banquet room. One story claims these are the bones of one of the Touhey brothers killed in a shootout. Another makes them to be that of someone who crossed the Touhey brothers in a business deal. Eddie Tuohey ran the bar while Roger owned and funded it. It was named The Wonder Bar until 1993 when it changed to The Bar Next Door. It was also Madison's first cigar bar.

The Investigation:

Upon arriving at the bar, Kristin Olshanski, gave us a quick tour. Derek and Troy drew a floor plan of all three floors for reference.

Alicia began observing and recording a time line of our activity of what we did and where. We began setting up our equipment on the second floor and basement as patrons still occupied the main floor.

Main floor set up and procedures:

(During closed hours and after customers left at approximately 9:00 p.m.)

(1) Three wireless surveillance cameras were placed on the main floor. One at the bottom of the stairwell closest to the front of the building facing up to the second floor, one on top of and at one end of the bar, and one near the front of the building facing toward the back end of the bar.
(2) Digital pictures were taken.
(3) Tri-Field Natural EMF Meter was placed.
(4) Deb performed the interview with bar manager, Kristin.

Second floor set up and procedures:

(1) The D.E.A.D. ® System was placed on the mantle of the fireplace closest to the back storage room and bathrooms.
(2) EMF sweeps, digital pictures and gauss readings were being performed. Ion counts were taken by Alicia and Dave.
(3) Laptop monitoring systems for Dave and Walt were in place.
(4) Jen, Troy and Deb were testing theories of slamming doors and moving chairs.
(5) Quiet observation was done in the dark for approximately 35 minutes
(6) Tim, Derek, Troy, Chris, and Dave performed E.V.P. later in the evening.

Basement set up and procedures:
Walt positioned his two motion detection cameras facing two different views for full coverage.

(1) Digital Camcorder was placed.
(2) Temperature Gauge was placed.
(3) Digital pictures were taken.

The Results:

Gauss Meter
Readings on the second floor varied between 400mG 1000mG. Normal non-paranormal Gauss meter readings range between 400-450mG.

Ion Counts
The negative and positive ion counts also varied on the second floor ranging between—400 to +150. During the data collection process, the positive ion count went from 50 ions/cm3 to 150 ions/cm3. The ion counts in the center of the room dropped to about ½ their value from 7:00pm to 7:45pm.

Non-Paranormal ranges have been reported to be between 400 and 450ions/cm3. Positive ions have been found to be associated with increased irritability and negative moods while negative ions have the opposite effects. Ions counts taken at location where there have been no reported paranormal events range between 400 and 450 ions/cm3 for both positive and negative ions.

Temperature
There were no abnormal temperature readings on any floors.

Pictures
There were no unusual pictures taken with digital or 35mm cameras.

Electronic Voice Phenomena (E.V.P.)
An E.V.P. was caught on audiotape during Deb's interview with Kristin. What is thought to be said is "Grandma" but the level of clarity is such that it is open to interpretation and can be varied. Visit our website at *www.investigatingthehaunted.com* to listen to the E.V.P. and draw your own conclusions.

EMF and Radiation Data

The graphs below show the EMF and radiation data. EMF data collection began at 6:14:31pm and ended at 9:11:15pm with 3176 data points collected. Radiation data collection began at 6:12:37pm and ended at 9:11:43pm with 178 data points collected.

The information below highlights the notable characteristics of the EMF data.

Time Period	Background	Spikes	Dips
6:14pm to 7:12pm	1.5mG	N/A	N/A
7:12pm to 7:40pm	0.8mG	2 to 6.5mG	N/A
7:40pm to 8:07pm	0.8mG	1 to 2mG	Down to 0mG
8:07pm to 9:11pm	0.2mG	1 to 2mG	Down to—.7mG

There was an interesting correlation found during the same time frame between a 'spiked' EMF point that Dave had recorded and a moving anomaly recorded in the basement by Walt. The gauss meter readings varied throughout the second floor from a low of 400mG to a high of 1000mG. The 1000mG reading in the center of the room in notable since Gauss meter readings of 400 to 450mG are normal and have been recorded in various locations where there are no reported paranormal events.

The decrease in 'background' and the first spike seen around 7:12pm correlate with a moving anomaly that was recorded in the basement by investigator Walt Baker.

THE SASSY HOUSE
Undisclosed Location
Watertown, WI

Date: September 3, 2005

Investigators: Derek Arneson, Troy Hartman, Jennifer Lauer, Karen Rowland, Dave Schumacher, and Nathan Thomas

Cause for Investigation:

The owner of the location contacted various members of the S.W.P.R.G. for help. She reported that strange occurrences have happened, such as: water bowls moving, phone being thrown off the charger, lights turning on and off, smell of strong urine and various other smells, cold spots, animals following things with their gaze, animals hiding or acting upset at unseen things, door knobs turning back and forth, doors opening, a dresser creaking, the owner's brother was dragged by the legs while sleeping, and the detection/sighting of various entities. The most concerning incident to the owner was the belief that there was an illegal spiritual taking of her dog.

The Investigation:

Set up and procedures:

Upon arriving at the location, there was a brief tour of the location for those who did not attend the pre-investigation. The equipment was set up and the investigation group split up into two teams.

1. Surveillance cameras were placed in the second floor bedroom, second floor main room, stairway to the second floor, and in the dining room/kitchen area. All video was captured on the DVR.
2. The D.E.A.D.© System for EMF, natural EMF temperature, and radiation was set up and run in the second floor bedroom and the second floor main room.
3. Ion counts, gauss meter readings, and radio frequency analysis was done on all floors and outside of the house.
4. The two teams did various data sweeps of their assigned areas. They recorded video, took pictures, measured temperature, EMFs, natural EMFs, and logged all data and personal observations.

5. E.V.P. sessions were conducted in the second floor bedroom and the second floor main room. A digital recorder was also left running in the second floor bedroom.

6. Quiet observation in the dark was done during various time throughout the night.

Results and Discussion:

Video

Nothing of note was seen on any of the video recorded.

Pictures

Nothing of note was seen in any of the pictures.

Ions

The table below shows the ion counts in various locations:

Location:	+ ions/cm3	—ions/cm3
Kitchen	120	300-800
Front entry	300	200-300
Basement	1000	800-900
Upstairs bedroom	50	200
Upstairs main room	500	400-500

* *'Normal' ion counts are usually in the +/- 500 ions/cm3.*
* *High concentrations of positive ions have been associated with irritability and negative moods while negative Ions have the opposite effect.*

Gauss meter (GMF)

Gauss meter readings of 400 to 600mG were recorded throughout various locations in the house. Normal readings are within the same range.

EMF

An EMF reading of 25 to 40mG was noted in the second floor bedroom closet. Investigators noted that outside power lines come over to the house at that location. There was an area in the main room on the second floor where the EMF reading would increase to 8 to 10mG for a few minutes and then return to 1 to 2mG. No definite source was located for these EMF readings.

The D.E.A.D.© System
(Direct Environmental Acquisition Data logging system)

- Triaxial ELF
  - ❖ There is an EMF 'spike' of 4.737mG at 8:13;14 PM in the second floor bedroom. This correlated with a radiation 'spike' of 25cpm.
  - ❖ The increase in EMF seen in the upstairs main room between 9:26:52pm and 9:34:54 correlates to the EMF increases that other investigators were reporting in that room. The equipment was later moved to the area where investigators reported the EMF increases. EMF readings of 8 to 9mG were recorded.
  - ❖ Unexplained 'spikes' in EMF have been reported in other locations where there are reports of paranormal experiences.

- Radiation
  - ❖ There was nothing of note for the upstairs main room.
  - ❖ There is a 'spike' of 25cpm at 8:14:40pm. This occurs within the same time frame as the EMF 'spike' noted above.
  - ❖ There is a 'dip' to 3cpm at 7:43:19pm. Nothing else happened at this time. Other researchers have noted drops in radiation in areas with reported paranormal activity.

- Temperature
  There was nothing of note for the ambient temperature readings taken at any of the locations.

Radio Frequency Analyzer
No frequencies were detected.

Investigator observations
During the pre-investigation on July 27th, 2005 a radio in the upstairs bedroom came on by itself. The second time investigators visited that room they noticed that the radio was on and was increasing in volume. They did not notice the radio being on the first time they were in the room. The video that was shot during the pre-investigation was reviewed and did confirm

that the radio was not on the first time the investigators were in the room but it was on the second time they were there.

E.V.P. Sessions

Two potential E.V.P. were recorded. The first occurred during the E.V.P. session in the upstairs bedroom. An investigator asked, "How old are you?" The second E.V.P. occurred while the digital recorder was left running in the upstairs bedroom. Two investigators were discussing equipment take down and a third voice was found upon review of the recording. It seems to be part of the conversation.

Visit the website *www.investigatingthehaunted.com* to listen to these E.V.P. and draw your own conclusions.

The Reveal:

Dave Schumacher and Jennifer Lauer returned to the residence on September 26, 2005 to reveal to the homeowner the information and data they collected. During the visit, while sitting at the kitchen table reviewing the two E.V.P. that were recorded, they clearly heard five or six distinctive footsteps on the 2nd floor. They more than just heard it . . . they felt the vibration of the footsteps.

Immediately, the two investigators and the homeowner ran upstairs . . . there was NO ONE THERE! The homeowner was very happy. She stated, "Finally, Someone else was here to hear that. This is what I've been experiencing myself."

Exclusive Report

Photo courtesy of Deb Skinvik

ROCKFORD REGISTER STAR
99 E. State Street
Rockford, IL

Date: October 12, 2005

Investigators: Chris Carter, Kyle Ford, Troy Hartman, Cindy Heinen, Jennifer Lauer, Kathy Santini-Richardson, Dave Schumacher, Deb Skinvik

Introduction and Background:

The S.W.P.R.G. was invited by the Rockford Register Star to conduct an investigation of the alleged haunting of the building that houses the newspaper. The newspaper was planning to do an article on the haunting and investigation for Halloween.

The building was built in 1932. It currently houses all aspects of the Rockford Register Star. It lies immediately next to the Rock River in downtown Rockford, IL.

There have been various reports of paranormal activity throughout the year in the tower. In the spring of 2000 Bea Ricotta, promotion specialist for the newspaper, reported hearing a woman's footsteps in the fifth floor storage area. In the fall of 2004, she heard something drop to the floor in a different storage area on the fifth floor. About ten years ago, another staffer reported seeing an apparition on the first floor near a copy machine. In addition, people have heard conversations on telephones in the basement between people who were not in the building. This occurred during and slightly after the renovation of the lunchroom. Others claim to have seen a ghost of a woman on the stairs going from the second floor to the pressroom.

The employees of the Rockford Register Star believe that the ghost could be that of the paper's ninth publisher, Ruth McCormick Simms. Ruth sporadically lived in the seventh-floor apartment until she died in 1944 at the age of 62. Ruth was the wife of U.S. Senator Medill McCormick, scion of the Chicago Tribune family. After Sen. McCormick's death, he married Arizona congressman, Albert Simms. Ruth achieved many accomplishments throughout her life, such as: an Illinois U.S. congresswoman, a radio station owner (KFLV, later WROK), and owner of a 2,400-acre Holstein cow farm in Byron.

The Investigation:

We did a pre-investigation visit of the location on October 3rd, 2005. We decided to set up the equipment on the main floor, fifth floor, and the seventh floor based on information obtained from the pre-investigation and baseline readings. Surveillance cameras (*IR DVR and DV cameras*) were placed throughout the areas mentioned above. The D.E.A.D.© System was set up and run on the main floor, fifth floor, and the seventh floor. Ion counts, gauss meter readings, and radio frequency analysis was done on the main floor, fifth floor, and seventh floor. Various data sweeps were done throughout the above-mentioned areas and in the basement lunchroom. Investigator personal experiences were recorded. E.V.P. sessions were conducted in the basement lunchroom and on the fifth and seventh floors.

Results and Discussion:

Video

Nothing of note was seen in any of the video footage.

Pictures

Nothing of note was seen in any of the pictures.

Ions

Ion counts ranged between 400 to 700 negative and positive ions/cm3. This is within the normal expected range.

Gauss meter (GMF)

Gauss meter readings of 500 to 700mG were recorded throughout various locations in the building. This is within the normal expected range.

EMF

Baseline EMFs were 0.8 to 1.4mG for the main floor, 1 to 4mG for the fifth floor, and 1 to 2.4 for the seventh floor. There were many 'spikes' on the fifth floor (see D.E.A.D.© section below).

Temperature Scans

There was nothing to note for the ambient temperature readings taken at any of the locations.

Radio Frequency Analyzer

A few frequencies were detected but none were dominant. There was a television-broadcasting studio in the building but it was not in use during the time of the investigation.

Investigator Observations

- Troy and Kyle experienced sweeping noises on the fifth floor at 8:19pm during quiet observation. There was also a strong, unpleasant odor coming from the bathroom in the fifth floor hallway, which was most likely sewer gas.
- Kathy viewed an unusual black beam during quiet observation at 7:46pm in the fifth floor bedroom, approximately 6 feet above the floor over the foot of the bed, started as a black 4-5 inch vertical line which then moved and extended around 8 inches in width (horizontal) getting shorter in length as movement occurred.
- Dave and Jen heard what sounded like a loud 'thud' on the fifth floor. They also heard what sounded like a box sliding on the floor. On the seventh floor, they heard what sounded like a door open and a few footsteps. Analysis of the video confirms that no one was present at the time the noises were heard.

Occurrences during E.V.P. sessions:

Seventh floor

- At 9:00pm Kathy was sitting by a monitor at a desk. The flash on her camera went dead and would not work for approximately 10 minutes. At this time a loud cracking noise happened above Kathy's head, which was heard by everyone sitting in the living room. Cindy believes this is on the E.V.P. tape.

Fifth floor

- At 9:30 PM Kathy and Bea, newspaper employee, heard a rustling in the corner of the room where the monitors were set-up. Immediately following this Deb, Cindy and Chris who were sitting in the hallway heard shuffling, rustling noises along with whispers. Upon hearing this Deb asked out loud if anyone else heard this. All heard whispering and Kyle states she heard someone say a distinct yes after Deb asked the group if anyone else heard the noises.

- We continued after this with quiet observation, whispering was heard again during this time. Kathy quietly walked over in the stairwell and elevator to make sure these noises were not coming from someone on the stairwell. It was determined that the only other people were Jen and Dave and they were upstairs on the seventh floor wrapping up equipment.

E.V.P.

Various E.V.P. were recorded on the fifth and seventh floors.

Visit the website *www.investigatingthehaunted.com* to listen to these E.V.P. and draw your own conclusions.

D.E.A.D.© System
(Direct Environmental Acquisition Data logging system)

The only interesting data were the EMFs and natural EMF from the fifth and seventh floors.

- The EMF levels on the fifth floor ranged between .956mG to 5.936mG. Pulses were seen between 3mG to 5mG (300nT to 500nT). The pulses occurred once every 4, 8, 18, 26, 28, 30, 32, or 34 seconds (which in hertz would be .25Hz, .125Hz, .05Hz, .04 Hz, .036Hz, .033Hz, .030Hz, and .029Hz). The majority happened once every 30 seconds (.033Hz).
- The EMF levels on the seventh floor ranged from .87mG to 18.67mG. There were two 'spikes' in the EMF: one at 8:33:51pm of 6.238mG and the second at 8:34:03pm of 18.67mG. There was also a 9.42uT 'spike' in the natural EMF that happened at 8:34:30pm. The other 'spikes' in the natural EMF was due to movement of the equipment or someone walking close to the equipment.

Conclusions:

This location produced many personal experiences, E.V.P., and interesting EMF data. The data is consistent with that collected at other locations where paranormal activity has been reported. It would be beneficial to revisit this location and collect more data.

THE ORCHARD HOUSE
Undisclosed Location
Burlington, WI

Date: August 6, 2005

Investigators: Walt Baker, Jennifer Lauer, Tara Razo, Alicia Sanders, Kathy Santini, Dave Schumacher, and Deb Skinvik

The homeowners are a brother & sister who will be referred to as, "Walt" and "Gloria"

Cause for Investigation:
The S.W.P.R.G. was contacted by the owners of the house. They had moved in one year ago. Since the move and renovation, they have been experiencing unexplained occurrences of: a toilet flushing, sounds of a bouncing ball under a bed, tapping on walls, voices, hearing a small electric fan going through a series of clicks and switching off by itself, a woman's voice telling the owner to "turn it off" (regarding the fan), small ball seen hopping and immediately stopping on its own on a wood floor hallway (making no sound), the smell of fresh flowers throughout the house, a shadow that looked like a male figure in a hallway, and an uncomfortable feeling that they shouldn't be in the basement.

The History:
The house is 40 yrs old. The land it sits on was once farmland. There have been four owners. Little is known about the house but upon a history check by the owners, they suspect a death may have occurred in the house. The last owner; an elderly lady named Annie, passed away of natural causes.

The Investigation:
Upon arriving at the house, the owner gave us a tour. It was a ranch style brick home with a closed in basement and large back yard and garage.

Set-up and procedures:
1. Surveillance cameras were placed in Walt's room, Gloria's room, the main hallway, and the entrance hallway. All video was captured on a DVR. A Sony handycam was placed in the basement.

2. D.E.A.D.© System (*Direct Environmental Acquisition Data logging system*) was set up and run in Walt's room, Gloria's room, and the basement.
3. Ion counts, gauss meter readings, and radio frequency analysis were done on all floors and outside of the house.
4. E.V.P. sessions were conducted in Gloria's room and the basement.

RESULTS AND DISCUSSION:

Video

After the investigation and upon review of the recorded video, it was noted that there were two times when the camera moved during the E.V.P. session in Gloria's room. This movement occurred shortly after an E.V.P. question "Can you show yourself?" The camera cord was securely wrapped around and fixed to a small table with the length of the cord running out of the bedroom and under the doorway (the door was closed) on the floor and into the kitchen for monitor hookup. No one was near the table or door when this happened. The camera movement appeared to be a small, quick, jerky motion to the right lasting for approximately 10 seconds. It stopped for almost three minutes and then continued again in a second small movement to the right for one second. The entire camera and base appeared to move as one unit. An additional camera that was stationed just outside the bedroom door into the hallway showed no one walking by the room or over the electrical cords. The camera does not move at all for the other four hours of recorded video. Note: This was also the same room where a woman's voice was heard by Gloria saying "turn it off!" (meaning for Gloria to turn off the small table fan). On another occasion, Gloria was in bed and could hear the fan clicking through a series of its switches from high to off on its own.

Ions

Ion counts were in the 400 to 500 ions/cm3 range throughout the location.

Gauss meter (GMF)

Gauss meter readings of 800 to 1000mG were recorded in the doorway of Walt's room and the hallway by Walt's room. The rest of the home had readings in the 350 to 500mG range and are similar to those locations where no paranormal experiences have been reported.

D.E.A.D.© System
(Direct Environmental Acquisition Data logging system)

- **Triaxial ELF**
  - ❖ The numerous EMF 'spikes' in the basement were most likely due to the wireless internet router that was located approximately 3 to 4 feet away
  - ❖ Two unexplained EMF 'spikes' of 4.3 and 3.5mG were seen in Walt's room *Unexplained 'spikes' in EMF have been reported in other locations where there are reports of paranormal experiences.*

- **Natural EMF**
  There was nothing of note for the natural EMF readings taken at any of the three locations.

- **Temperature**
  There was nothing of note for the ambient temperature readings taken at any of the three locations.

- **Radiation**
  - ❖ The relatively high 25cpm reading in Walt's room occurs at the same time that the 4.3 and 3.5mG EMF 'spikes' was recorded. However, due to the high variability of the radiation readings and the numerous other 'spikes' in the radiation, this could simply be a chance finding.

Radio Frequency Analyzer
There were no frequencies noted.

E.V.P. Sessions
Gloria's Room

- **E.V.P. #1**
- Something was heard after Deb asked, "What is your name?"

- **E.V.P. #2**
- Deb asked the following question, "Can you show yourself?" A few seconds later a bang and scratch were heard from the bedroom

wall facing the backyard. Dave was sitting on the floor with his back against the wall. The sound, which was heard by all people in the room, came from just above his head. This sound was recorded and can easily be heard. A possible E.V.P. was discovered upon review of the recorded session. Immediately following the bang and scratch there is an E.V.P. which sounds like, "You bet ya."

- **E.V.P. 3**
- Something was captured right after the fan was turned off.

Visit our website: *www.investigatingthehaunted.com* to listen to the E.V.P.

Conclusion:

Explained EMF spikes, camera movement, and interesting E.V.P. have raised questions regarding the reported paranormal activity within this house. It has been speculated by the owners that the voices heard and other unexplained activity could be that of Annie, the previous owner. This remains undetermined.

THE PARK HOUSE HAUNTING
Undisclosed Location
Sun Prairie, WI

Date: April 29, 2006

Investigators: Walt Baker, Jennifer Lauer, Dave Schumacher, and Deb Skinvik

Cause for Investigation:

The owners of this location contacted the S.W.P.R.G. about some strange experiences they have had in their home. They reported odd odors coming from the closet in the master bedroom on several occasions, strange electrical power draws, feelings of a presence in the upstairs and computer room areas on the first floor, and several sightings of the apparition of a small boy residing in the upstairs area of the home. The owners stated that the boy seemed to run back and forth between the two upper bedrooms on the second floor. Stories of a boy who had shot himself in the head with a pistol had been told to us by the owner but were not confirmed. Everyone in the house has witnessed these occurrences several times. The house had even been rented out for several years and the renters had all claimed to see this boy.

Pre-Investigation Information:

On April 27th, 2006 S.W.P.R.G. investigators Derek Arneson, Troy Hartman, & Jennifer Lauer conducted a pre-investigation of the home. The pre-investigation consisted of talking with the homeowners and other witnesses of the reported paranormal activity occurring in the home. A tour of the home, baseline readings and a debunking process then took place. The homeowner had reported experiencing a high power draw from a piece of equipment he had brought into the home prior to us arriving that night.

During our two hour pre-investigation, one of our investigator's video camera went dead only after a few minutes with a fully charged battery. Another investigator's camera and cell phone batteries were completely drained as well. A high EMF pulse was noted in the downstairs computer room area. Nothing else of interest was noted during the pre-investigation.

THE INVESTIGATION:

Set up and procedures:
The IR video cameras with the DVR system were placed in the stairway, upstairs hallway, and in the two upstairs bedroom.

The D.E.A.D.© system was run in the living room, kitchen, bottom of the stairs, and in the two upstairs bedrooms.

Data sweeps and E.V.P. were done throughout the location.

RESULTS AND DISCUSSION:

Video
Nothing of note was seen on any of the video recorded.

Pictures
Nothing of note was seen in any of the pictures.

Radio Frequency Analyzer
No frequencies were detected.

D.E.A.D.© System
(Direct Environmental Acquisition Data logging system)

1. The owner and an S.W.P.R.G. investigator were in the small upstairs bedroom, referred to as the Children's Room, when they both heard someone say, "Hey."
2. Two investigators asked, "Can you show yourself to us?" A voice saying, "Yes" was heard by the investigators who were the only people in the room at that time.
3. A whimpering sound was heard by three of the six people in the room.
4. There was a large 'spike' in the EMF of 267mG when the owner attempted to antagonize whatever was there.

The graph below (Power) shows the EMF data collected during the times that the above events occurred. The numbers above the 'spikes' on the graph correlate with the numbered events above.

During an E.V.P. session, when the main power to the house was shut off, one of the S.W.P.R.G. investigators had the sensation of being poked in the back and another investigator experienced the sensation of a thump to the right temple of their head. The owner of the home felt a child's arms wrap around his leg. There was a 287mG 'spike' recorded only during the time that all of this happened (No Power).

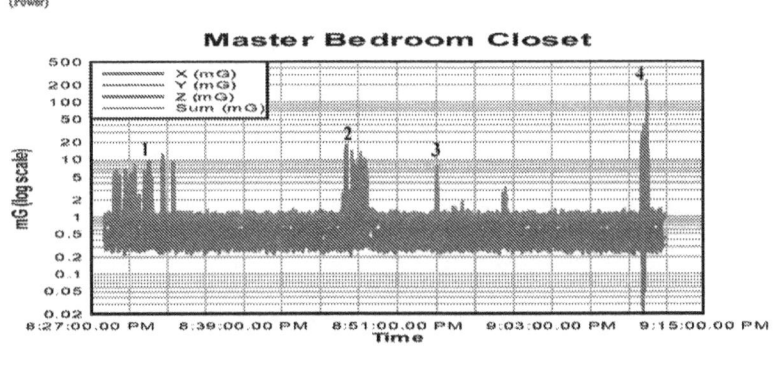

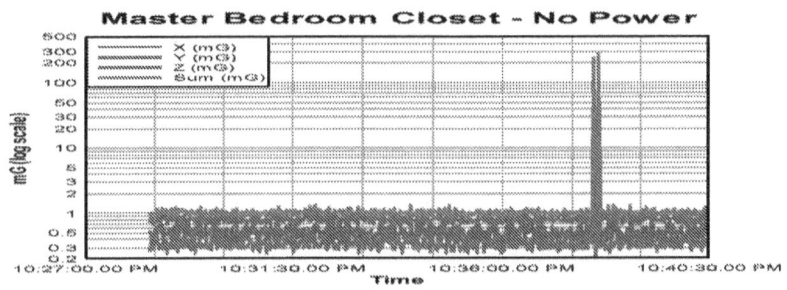

E.V.P. Sessions

No E.V.P. were found on any of the recordings.

Investigator Experiences

S.W.P.R.G. investigator Dave Schumacher experienced a 'cold spot.' It was a bone chilling cold feeling that happened for about two minutes. There was no change detected in the ambient air temperature but there was an increase in the positive ion count from 300 ions/cm3 to 3000 ions/cm3 during this experience. Once the experience was over the ion counts returned to their low levels.

Conclusion:

The various audio and other personal experiences had by the investigators and owners correlated with changes in the EMF field and ion counts. No natural explanations for these changes and occurrences could be found. This data is consistent with that collected in other locations with reported paranormal activity.

Section VII

REFERENCES AND FURTHER READING
AND INFORMATION

References

CHAPTER 5

1. Tyrell (1943). Apparitions. Society for Psychical Research. London, UK.
2. Roll & Persinger (2001). In J. Houran & R. Lange (Eds.), Hauntings and Poltergeists: Multidisciplinary Perspectives. Jefferson, NC. McFarland & Co., Inc. pp.123-163.
3. Gearhart & Persinger (1986). Perceptual and Motor Skills, 6, 463-466.
4. Roll & Gearhart (1974). In R.L. Morris & J. Morris (Eds.), Research in Parapsychology 1973. Metuchen, NJ. Scarecrow. pp.44-46.
5. Roll (1977). Poltergeists. In B.B. Wolman (Ed.), Handbook of Parapsychology. New York, NY. Van Nostrand Reinhold Company. pp.577-630.
6. Solfvin & Roll (1976). In J.D. Morris, W.G. Roll, & R.L. Morris (Eds.), Research in Parapsychology 1975. Metuchen, NJ. Scarecrow. pp.115-120.
7. Makarec & Persinger (1985). Perceptual and Motor Skills, 60, 831-834.
8. Persinger (1984). Perceptual and Motor Skills, 59, 583-586.
9. Budden (1998). Electric UFOs:Fireballs, Electromagnetic and Abnormal States. London, UK. Blandford.
10. Persinger (1985). Perceptual and Motor Skills, 61, 320-322.
11. Persinger (1987). Journal of the American Society for Psychical Research, 81, 23-36.
12. Persinger (1989). Neuroscience Letters, 88, 271-274.
13. Persinger (1989). In L.A. Henkel & R.E. Berger (Eds.), Research in Parapsychology 1988. Metuchen, NJ. Scarecrow. pp121-156.
14. Gauld (1977). In B.B. Wolman (Ed.), Handbook of Parapsychology. New York, NY. Van Nostrand Reinhold Company. pp.577-630.
15. Collins (1948). The Cheltenham Ghosts. London, UK. Psychic Press.

16. Roll (1994). In D.J. Bierman (Ed.), Proceedings of Presented Papers 37th Annual Convention of the Parapsychological Association. University of Amsterdam, August 7-10, 1994. pp.347-351.

17. Roney-Dougal (1993). Where science and magic meet. Rockport, MA. Element Inc.

18. Houran & Lange (1996). Perceptual and Motor Skills, 83, 499-502.

19. MacDonald (1970). Psychological Reports, 26, 791-798.

20. Houran & Lange (1996). Perceptual and Motor Skills, 83, 365-366.

21. Budner (1962). Journal of Personality, 30, 29-50.

22. Schwartz & Creath (2005). Journal of Scientific Exploration, 19(3), 343-358.

23. Wood (2007). PSI Journal of Investigative Psychical Research, 3(1), 10-18.

24. Hannemyr (2007). Imaging Defects: Blooming URL *http://hannemyr. com/photo/defects.html#bloom*

25. UKParanormal (2007). Orbs, what the hell are they? URL *http://www. ukparanormal.co.uk/Orbs.html*

26. *http://www.p-s-i.org.uk/orbs-2-1.htm*

27. Wood (2005). Journal of Investigative Psychical Research, 1(1), 10-15.

CHAPTER 6

1. *www.ghostgadgets.com/_knowledge/emfmeters.html*

2. Townsend (2004). Journal of the Association for the Scientific Study of Anomalous Phenomena. 35, 2-20.

3. Braithwaite & Townsend (2005). European Journal of Parapsychology. 20, 65-78.

4. Schumacher & Carter (2006). Haunted Times. Vol. 1 Issue 4, 48-49.

5. Roll & Persinger (2001). In Hauntings and Poltergeists: Multidisciplinary Perspectives. Eds. James Houran & Rense Lange. McFarland & Company, Inc. Jefferson, NC. 123-163.

6. Charry & Hawkinshire (1981). Journal of Personality and Social Psychology. 41, 185-197.

CHAPTER 7

1. Bell et al (1992). Electroenceph. & Clin. Neurophys, 83, 389-397.

2. Bell et al (1994). J. of Neurosci, 123, 26-32.

3. Cook & Persinger (2001). Percep. & Motor Skills, 2, 447-448.

4. Fuller et al (1995). Brain Res. Bull., 36, 155-159.

5. Gearhart & Persinger (1986). Percep. & Motor Skills, 62, 463-466.

6. Papi et al (1995). Bioelectromagnetics, 3, 341-347.
7. Persinger et at (1973). Percep. & Motor Skills, 36, 1131-1157.
8. Persinger (1988). Neurosci. Lett., 88, 271-274.
9. Persinger (1993). Percep. & Motor Skills, 76, 444-446.
10. Persinger & Koren (2001). Hauntings & Poltergeists: Multidisciplinary Perspective (H&P:MP) 179-194.
11. Randall & Randall (1991). Biolelectromagnetics, 12, 67-70.
12. Roll & Persinger (2001). H&P:MP 123-163.
13. Persinger et al (2001). Percep. & Motor Skills, 3, 673-674.
14. Persinger & Richards (1994). Percep. & Motor Skills, 79, 1571-1578.
15. Persinger et al (1977). Percep. & Motor Skills, 84, 527-536.
16. Persinger (1999). Int. J. of Parapsych., 34, 163-169.
17. Persinger (1995). Percep. & Motor Skills, 80, 563-569.
18. Nichols & Roll (1999). Proc. Presented Papers: The Parapsych. Assoc. 42nd Ann. Conv.
19. Roll & Nichols (1998) Proc. Presented Papers: The Parapsych. Assoc. 39th Ann. Conv.
20. Nichols & Roll (1998).) Proc. Presented Papers: The Parapsych. Assoc. 41st Ann. Conv.
21. Roll et al (1992).). Proc. Presented Papers: The Parapsych. Assoc. 35th Ann. Conv.
22. Persinger & Cameron (1986). J. Am. Soc. Psych. Res., 61, 49-73.
23. Wiseman et al (2002). J. Parapsych., 66, 387-408.
24. Wiseman et al (2003). Brit. J. Psych., 94, 195-211.
25. Braithwaite (2004). E. J. Parapsych., 19, 3-28.
26. Braithwaite & Townsend (2005). E. J. Parapsych, 20.1, 65-78.
27. Persinger et al (1973). Percep. & Motor Skills, 36, 1131-1159.
28. Houran (2000). J. Soc. Psy. Res., 64, 141-158.
29. Lange & Houran (1997). Percep. & Motor Skills, 84, 1455-1458.
30. Lange & Houran (2001). H&P:MP 280-306.
31. McCue (2002). J. Soc. Psychical Res., 66 (866), 1-21.
32. Budden (1998). Electric UFOs: Fireballs, Electromagnetic and Abnormal States.
33. Budden (1999). Psychic Close Encounters.
34. Tyrell (1973). Apparitions. First published in 1943.
35. Radin (2001). H&P:MP 164-178.
36. Maker & Hansen (1997). Proc. Presented Papers: The Parapsych. Assoc. 40th Ann. Conf.
37. Maker (2000). J. Parapsych., 63, 47-80.

38. Rajaram & Mitra (1981). Neuro. Sci. Let., 24, 187-191.
39. Persinger, M.A. (1988). Neuro. Sci. Let., 88, 271-274.
40. Horowitz, M.J. & Adams, J.E. (1970). Origins and mechanisms of hallucination. New York: Plenum Press. 13-20.
41. Booth, J.N., Koren, S.A., & Persinger, M.A. (2005). Int. J. Neurosci., 115, 1053-1079.
42. Persinger et al. (2000). Percept. & Motor Skills, 90, 659-674.
43. Cook & Persinger (1997). Percept & Motor Skills, 85, 683-693.

CHAPTER 8

1. Auerbach, Loyd. *Ghost Hunting: How To Investigate the Paranormal.* Berkeley, California: Ronin Publishing, 2004.
2. Belanger, Jeff. *Communicating With the Dead: Reach Beyond the Grave.* Franklin Lake, New Jersey: Career Press, 2005.
3. Bion, Stephen. "Software: E.V.P.maker." *Willkommen: und viel Spaß auf meinen Webseiten!* 28 June 2006.
4. *http://stefanbion.de/evpmaker/index_e.htm*
5. Boylan, Grace Duffie. *Thy Son Liveth: Messages From a Soldier to His Mother.* Boston: Little, Brown and Company, 1918.
6. Butler, Tom. "Formation of Electronic Phenomena." *Metaphysical Concepts.* 2006. 29 June 2006.
7. *http://ethericreality.aaevp.com/concepts.htm*
8. Butler, Tom and Lisa Butler. "4Cell E.V.P. Demonstration" *American Association of Electronic Voice Phenomena.* 08 June 2006. 29 June 2006 *http://www.aaevp.com/articles/articles_about_4cell_experiment.htm*
9. Butler, Tom and Lisa Butler. *There is No Death and There Are No Dead.* Reno, Nevada: AAEVP Publishing, 2004.
10. Carroll, Robert T. "Pareidol." *The Skeptic's Dictionary.* 2006. 18 May 2006 *http://skepdic.com/pareidol.html*
11. Chisholm, Judith. *Voices From Paradise: How the Dead Speak To Us.* Charlbury, England: Jon Carpenter Publishing, 2000.
12. Eisenbud, Jules. *The World of Ted Serios: Thoughtographic Studies of an Extraordinary Mind.* New York: William Morrow & Company, 1967.
13. Estep, Sarah Wilson. *Voices of Eternity.* New York: Fawcett Gold Medal Press, 1988.
14. Gunnlaugsson, Olafur. "Compact Cassette." *Audiotools.com.* 2005. 18 May 2006 *http://audiotools.com/cass.html*

15. Heinen, Cindy and Dave Schumacher. "Electronic Voice Phenomena and Local Sidereal Time: A Pilot Study". Journal of Paranormal Research. In press.

16. "How it Works: Losin' it." *Deafening Sound.* 2000. NETonline. 27 June 2006. *http://net.unl.edu/artsFeat/deafening_sound/ds_losin_it.html*

17. Juergenson, Friedrich. *Voice Transmissions with The Deceased.* 1964. Trans. Thomas Wingert and George Wynne. Sweden: Friedrich Juergenson Foundation. 2001. *http://www.fargfabriken.se/fjf*

18. Konstantinos. *Speak With the Dead: Seven Methods of Spirit Communication.* St. Paul, Minnesota: Llewellyn Publishing, 2004.

19. Kubis, Pat and Mark Macy. *Conversations Beyond the Light With Departed Friends and Colleagues by Electronic Means.* Boulder, Colorado: Griffin Publishing, 1995.

20. Locher, Theo and Maggy Harsch-Fishbach. *Breakthroughs in Technical Spirit Communication.* Trans. Hans Heckmann. Boulder, Colorado: Continuing Life Research, 1997.

21. Macy, Mark H. *Miracles in the Storm.* New York: New American Library, 2001

22. Macy, Mark H. "The Phenomenal History and Future of ITC Research— Gemelli." *World ITC: The New Technology of Spiritual Contact.* July 2006. 20 May 2006 *http://www.worlditc.org/a_02_macy_itc_history.htm#Gemelli*

23. MacRae, Alexander. *E.V.P. and New Dimensions.* Sanctuary Press, 2004.

24. MacRae, Alexander. "Experiment 1." *Skyelab.* 27 June 2006 *http://www.skyelab.co.uk/expt1.htm*

25. "NASA's New Spaceships." *National Aeronautics and Space Administration.* 30 June 2006. 30 July 2006 *http://www.nasa.gov/mission_pages/exploration/spacecraft/ares_naming.html*

26. "Noise-Induced Hearing Loss (NIHL)." *House Ear Institute: Fact Sheet.* House Ear Institute. 27 June 2006 *http://www.hei.org/news/facts/nihlfact.htm*

27. Presi, Paolo. "Curriculum Vitae: Paolo Presi." *World ITC: The New Technology of Spiritual Contact.* 26 June 2006 *http://www.worlditc.org/h_01_vitae_presi.htm*

28. Radin, Dean. "A Dog That Seems to Know When His Owner Is Coming Home: Effects of Geomagnetism and Local Sidereal Time." *Boundary Institute.* 2000. 10 July 2006 *http://www.boundaryinstitute.org/articles/jaytee2.pdf*

29. Ratnikas, Algis. "Timeline 1959" *Timelines in History.* 29 July 2006 *http://timelines.ws/20thcent/1959.html*

30. Raudive, Konstantin. *Breakthrough: An Amazing Experiment in Electronic Communication with the Dead.* Trans. Nadia Fowler. Gerrards Cross, England: Colin Smythe, 1971.

31. Schooner, Steve. "From Stereo to Cassette." *Magnetic Tape Recording Invented.* 2005. 18 May 2006

32. *http://history.acusd.edu/gen/recording/notes.html*

33. Schoenherr, Steve. "Origins." *Magnetic Tape Recording Invented.* 2005. 18 May 2006 *http://history.acusd.edu/gen/recording/notes.html*

34. Schumacher, Dave, Cindy Heinen and Chris Carter. "E.V.P. and Geomagnetic Fields: Is There a Correlation?" *AAEVP* 11 November 2006 *http:www.aaevp. com/research/research_geomagnetic_fields.htm*

35. Spottiswoode, James P. "Apparent Association Between Effect Size in Free Response Anomalous Cognition Experiments and Local Sidereal Time." *The Journal of Scientific Exploration* 11.2 (1997). 10 July 2006 *http://www. jsasoc.com/docs/JSE-LST.pdf*

Resources

AUDIO PROGRAMS

AVS Audio Tools: *http://www.avsmedia.com/AudioTools/index.aspx*

Acoustic: *http://www.acoustica.com*

Adobe Audition: *http://www.adobe.com/products/audition/index.html*

Amazing Slow Downer: *http://www.ronimusic.com*

Audacity: *http://audacity.sourceforge.net*

Clear Voice Denoiser: *http://www.speechpro.com/production/?fid=7&id=468*

DC Six Audio Work Station: *http://www.tracertek.com/dc_six.htm*

Goldwave: *http://www.goldwave.com*

BOOKS

Butler, Tom and Lisa Butler. *"There is No Death and There Are No Dead"* Reno, Nevada: AA-E.V.P. Publishing, 2004.

Konstantinos. *"Speak With the Dead: Seven Methods of Spirit Communication"* St. Paul, Minnesota: Llewellyn Publishing, 2004.

DOWNLOADS

Bion, Stefan ~ E.V.P.maker: *http://stefanbion.de/evpmaker/index_e.htm*

MacRae, Alexander ~ The Sounds of E.V.P.: h*ttp://www.lulu.com/EVP*

Rinaldi, Sonia ~ Portuguese Crowd Babble: *http://aaevp.com/resources/resources2.htm#Background_Sound*

www.ingramcontent.com/pod-product-compliance
Lightning Source LLC
Chambersburg PA
CBHW020918290526
45784CB00002BA/600